11/2, [illegible]

To Jerry &
Cheyenne,

MONEY
MEDITATIONS
for Women

Live Long &
Prosper —

Joan
Sordahl

MONEY MEDITATIONS
for Women

THOUGHTS, EXERCISES, RESOURCES, AND
AFFIRMATIONS FOR CREATING PROSPERITY

JO ANN LORDAHL, Ph.D.

CELESTIAL ARTS
Berkeley, California

CELESTIAL ARTS PUBLISHING
P.O. Box 7123
Berkeley, CA 94707

Cover and text designs by Nancy Austin and Toni Tajima

Front cover photography by Jonathan Chester / Extreme Images

Library of Congress Cataloging-in-Publication Data

Lordahl, Jo Ann
    Money meditations for women / by Jo Ann Lordahl.
       p.   cm.
    Includes bibliographical references.
    ISBN 0-89087-694-0
    1. Women—Finance, Personal.   2. Finance, Personal—Religious aspects.   3. Money—Religious aspects.   4. Work and family.
5. Meditations. I. Title.
HG179.L575   1993
332.024′042—dc20
                               93-16496
                               CIP

FIRST PRINTING 1994

Printed in the United States of America

   2   3   4   5 — 98   97   96

CONTENTS

INTRODUCTION

Money Meditations for Women is a book to help you improve your relationship with money and create prosperity in your life, and perhaps to rethink money's relationship with spirituality. It is a know-yourself guide to financial empowerment and is packed with resources, spiritual and motivational ideas, tactics, suggestions and information.

The roots of *Money Meditations for Women* reach deep into my personal history. At its simplest—and no money history is simple—my father, with inherited wealth, spent money as if it would always be there. The inheritance evaporated long before my childhood was over. My mother, whose ingrained southern morality rather considered money to be evil, managed to become a superb bargain hunter, saleoholic, and pack rat.

The lessons of life's financial uncertainty were brought home to me still further over the years as I counselled, hired, and talked with many women, first as a personnel clerk and then later as director for a company hiring mostly women for both part- and full-time jobs. The memory of the hurt and shocked woman in her forties who lost husband and livelihood to a younger woman lives with me still. Nor can I forget the brave older woman, fired but still leaving home every day as if she had a job because she couldn't bear to tell the sister dependant on her for support.

In *Money Meditations for Women* I share insights both from a wealth of books and articles and from the experiences of myself, my friends, and the many women I have encountered in my professional life.

To help you concentrate where you choose, there are three sections: (1) *Creating your Financial Future,* (2) *Learning to Manage Your*

Money, and (3) *Creating Prosperity.* This division is fluid, for a single meditation may speak to many issues.

Part I, *Creating Your Financial Future,* gives inspiration for changing our ideas and attitudes toward our financial independence and other issues we have around money. It shows us how we can use affirmations to create the financial future we desire.

Part II, *Learning to Manage Your Money,* contains tips, ideas, warnings, and strategies for better money management.

Part III, *Creating Prosperity,* reveals money as a spiritual tool, and contains ideas of being a caretaker of all our resources.

This book saves you time by consolidating resources and ideas. Throughout the book you will find quotes, meditations, exercises, and affirmations that center on the three themes above. For your convenience, references are listed on each page; at the end of *Money Meditations for Women* there is also a selected list of books that will help you explore many of these issues of money, empowerment, and spirituality in more depth.

Money Meditations for Women is meant to be used. Write in it, turn down pages, or loan it to a friend. You may choose to read *Money Meditations for Women* all at once, but remember, these daily meditations cover an entire year. Never be overwhelmed. Skip around, skim, or stay with a thought, page, or section until you're ready to move on. Some money ideas and habits will change overnight. Other financial changes will require more persistence. Mark your progress year by year as well as day by day. You will seize some ideas quickly and run with them. Others will not apply to your circumstances, or not apply to them right now. Still others will come to you as calmly as old friends, changing your life when you least expect.

I hope that *Money Meditations for Women* nurtures your search for financial wellness and spiritual growth, whatever form that search takes. You and I and our friends are literally making new places in the world by sharing our courage, joy, resources, and spiritual values. Together our possibilities have no end.

CREATING YOUR
FINANCIAL FUTURE

Too often we know what we want to do but never seem to begin to do it. When our thoughts and talk outdistance our actions we can use affirmations to help us close this gap between dreams and reality. This section helps us use affirmations to identify and change our attitudes to money, and to inspire us toward financial independence.

Affirmations are simple yet powerful tools. Prescott Lecky's *Self-Consistency* gives us the principle that affirmations work on: Convince your mind something is true and your behavior will follow tamely.

Over twenty years ago, without putting a name to what I was doing, I used affirmations to stop my three-pack-a-day smoking habit. About two weeks before I planned to quit, I began saying to myself, "I am a person who does not smoke."

I felt a struggle in my mind between opposing voices. When I would say, "I, Jo Ann, am a person who doesn't smoke," a loud voice would yell, "You do so smoke!" However, I continued to repeat over and over what I wanted to be true. Two weeks later, I *was* a person who did not smoke, and, with some effort, I've remained one.

I never called this change agent *affirmations* and, strangely, I forgot all about this powerful tool. A long time later, struggling to raise my self-esteem out of the cellar, I used a new affirmation that I found in Sandra Orr's *Rebirthing:* "I, Jo Ann, am a lovable person." I would write out ten statements in each of three voices, "I, Jo Ann…," "You, Jo Ann…," and "She, Jo Ann…,"—when I had finished writing, my hand would actually ache: So far was the distance between my negative unconscious beliefs and the new, self-loving person I wanted to be. Making this change took years.

With affirmations we can erase old thought patterns and reinvent our lives. In a deeper sense, affirmations allow us to align ourselves with larger, universal patterns. We are better able to be in the right place, at the right time, with the right people, doing what we most need to—which may not be exactly what we had planned for ourselves. We may even discover we have been wishing for the wrong thing, and then go on to find new affirmations and a new life that suits us better.

Make the affirmations your own: If you need to, rewrite them so they fit your needs. Perhaps you'll work with a new one each day, or maybe you'll stay with one until you feel a shift begin to happen.

When you work with an affirmation, repeat it to yourself as often as possible, particularly during those times when you're feeling inwardly centered: after meditation or prayer, awakening in the middle of the night, in the morning following exercise or yoga, or in the middle of a pleasant daydream. You can say them silently or out loud when appropriate, or write them, or read them from a card. The unconsious mind will eventually work to make the affirmation a part of your waking reality, so stick with it and remember: AFFIRMING WHO YOU ARE HELPS YOU TO BECOME WHAT YOU WANT TO BE.

DAY 1

Every woman has the power to create her own future. With proper planning and choices, she can realize objectives and goals she never dreamed possible. You can be that woman.

JUDITH MARTINDALE & MARY MOSES*

Self-control is a valuable commodity. Not eating the extra cookie, saving money in a workable plan, walking every day: these build self-control.

Think of self-control as a muscle that grows strong when you exercise it and weak when you don't!

AFFIRMATION

Through planning and choice I create the financial future I want.

---

* Judith A. Martindale and Mary J. Moses, *Creating Your Own Future* (Naperville, IL: Sourcebooks Trade, 1991).

DAY 2

A change in your behavior first thing in the morning demonstrates that you have made a commitment to change your life.

MARTIN KATAHN[*]

Most of us have constructed our lives so that there's little spare time. Outside events usually beckon so loudly that the quiet inner voices murmuring that our finances are a mess are drowned before we hear them.

One tactic to help accomplish change is to make and prioritize "To Do" lists. Also, turn your new activities into routines—these routines become as easy as saving your dimes in a vase every day.

Exercise: Do your chosen new behavior first thing in the morning when you and the day are fresh with new possibilities.

AFFIRMATION

I am in control of my financial life.

---

[*] Martin Katahn, *The 200 Calorie Solution: How To Burn An Extra 200 Calories A Day And Stop Dieting* (New York: Norton, 1982).

DAY 3

In educating oneself it is best to root out bad habits and tolerate those that are harmless.

The I Ching: Or Book of Changes*

The reason why almost half of this book about money is devoted to motivating and working with ourselves is that at least half of the origins of our financial problems are located within ourselves. Vast progress comes from being able to accept that we have control over our own problems.

AFFIRMATION

I gently and lovingly root out those habits that harm my financial and personal well-being.

* *The I Ching: Or Book of Changes*, the Richard Wilhelm Translation (Princeton, NJ: Princeton University Press, 1950).

DAY 4

Fear is always our sign to pay attention. Sometimes fear reminds us that we need to save more money, pay bills or accumulate experience before moving toward the life we say we want.

MARSHA SINETAR*

"Anxiety...can be alleviated only if it is de-mystified," says Carol Becker in her book, *The Invisible Drama: Women and the Anxiety of Change.*

Paying attention to our fears and anxieties and then getting them under control will help us in dealing with our financial lives. Different methods work for different people. "Write into your fear," a writer friend used to tell me. "Write about what you're afraid of, do what you're afraid of."

When I cannot do something, there is always a reason. Better results come when I pay attention to my resistance than when I attempt to ignore it.

AFFIRMATION

I pay attention to my financial fears and move through them.

---

* Marsha Sinetar, *A Way Without Words: A Guide for Spiritually Emerging Adults* (Mahwah, NJ: Paulist Press, 1992).

DAY 5

In our time and culture, the battlefield of life is money. But the inner enemies remain the same now as they were in ancient India or feudal Japan: fear, self-deception, vanity, egoism, wishful thinking, tension, and violence.

JACOB NEEDLEMAN[*]

In this book, we are taking up a path with a purpose: integrating spirituality and money. A lot of what we gain from our path will be in the doing: we gain self-discipline, concentration, and the ability to defer immediate gratification in the interest of long-term goals. We work at speaking up for our best interest, at judging the truthfulness and worth of others, at understanding ourselves, and at distinguishing between our *needs* and our *wants*.

In the battle to understand and control money in our lives, we remain aware of Needleman's inner enemies: "fear, self-deception, vanity, egoism, wishful thinking, tension, and violence."

AFFIRMATION

In understanding and controlling my finances I learn to tame my inner enemies.

---

[*] Jacob Needleman, *Money and the Meaning of Life* (New York: Doubleday, 1991).

DAY 6

Take stock of your life this very day. Sit down quietly by yourself with a pencil and paper, and write down the three things that you most wish for in life.…Be specific, not vague. Then write down underneath three things or conditions that you wish to remove from your life. Again, be definite and specific, and not vague.

EMMET FOX*

    Religious leader Emmet Fox continues by telling us to take each of these six things and, for a few minutes, to bring all our spiritual and metaphysical knowledge to bear on them. He tells us to repeat this treatment of our six-item list every single day for the next month.

> Claim gently but definitely that the Great Creative Life Force of the Universe is bringing each of the first three things into your life in Its own way, in Its own time, and in Its own form. Then claim that the same Great Power is dissolving each of the latter three, also in Its own way.

Fox tells us not to dictate the exact terms or be vehement or impatient, and to keep our use of affirmations private.

AFFIRMATION
I use my personal power to improve my life and my finances.

---

* Emmet Fox, *Alter Your Life* (New York: Harper, 1931).

DAY 7

You are a living magnet, constantly drawing to you the things, the people, and the circumstances that are in accord with your thoughts. In other words, you are where you are in experience, in relationships, even in financial conditions, because of what you are (which is where you are in consciousness).

ERIC BUTTERWORTH*

Coming to believe that my thoughts affect my possibilities has been a long process. My attitude was first changed when I read a psychological study about success rates in reading the backs of cards. In this study, the "goats" (those who believed they had no psychic powers) performed as negatively as the "sheep" (those who thought they had psychic powers) performed positively. In other words, if people thought they had psychic powers, they had them; if they knew they didn't have psychic powers, sure enough, they didn't!

AFFIRMATION

As I increase the prosperity of my thoughts I increase my financial well-being.

---

* Eric Butterworth, *Spiritual Economics: The Prosperity Process* (Unity Village, MO: Unity School of Christianity, 1983).

DAY 8

You have to be willing to throw out what doesn't work—no matter how many experts recommend it—and stick with what really improves your life and makes you feel better about yourself....

The point is that you need to take the information and translate it into a system that works for you.

SUSAN POWTER*

AFFIRMATION

I create financial systems that work for me.

* "Susan Powter's Secrets of Getting Motivated, Staying Motivated,"
  Bottom Line, April 1994.

DAY 9

Many scoff when they first encounter the idea of affirmations. So did I. But on the other hand, I eventually decided, a closed mind has never been the hallmark of a functioning intelligence. Today I employ affirmations regularly; I'm enough of a pragmatist to use what works.

JERROLD MUNDIS[*]

AFFIRMATION

I use affirmations to increase my financial prosperity.

---

[*] Jerrold Mundis, *How to Get Out of Debt, Stay Out of Debt and Live Prosperously* (New York: Bantam Books, 1988).

DAY 10

A good way to get started is to choose only one new habit and practice it without fail for three weeks. It normally takes three weeks for a new habit to feel comfortable. Once you're comfortable with the new habit, choose another, practice it for three weeks, choose another, and so on. Soon you'll find yourself getting a lot more done with a lot less stress. It's also very important that you begin immediately. If you wait until you feel inspired to begin, you'll wait forever. Just act the way you want to be and soon you'll be the way you act.

MICHAEL LEBOEUF*

Exercise: Today write your chosen affirmation on a card and carry it around with you.

AFFIRMATION

_____

_____

---

* Michael LeBoeuf, *Fast Forward* (New York: G. P. Putnam's, 1993).

DAY 11

Money is a limited resource. As we all know, it never really buys lasting freedom, security, love, and power, but only a temporary facsimile of those states. To feel really free, secure, loving, and powerful requires emotional maturity, an integrated sense of personal value that money cannot buy.

VICTORIA FELTON-COLLINS*

Gaining maturity, learning how to really live and enjoy life, learning money's value—what it can buy for us and what it can't—these are lifetime propositions. There are no shortcuts. We simply have to learn from our own life experience and what we glean from others.

AFFIRMATION

Every day in every way I grow more wise.

---

* Victoria Felton-Collins, *Couples and Money: Why Money Interferes with Love and What to Do About it* (New York: Bantam Books, 1990).

DAY 12

No woman can attract money if she despises it. Many people are kept in poverty by saying: "Money means nothing to me, and I have a contempt for people who have it."

FLORENCE SCOVEL SHINN*

AFFIRMATION

I have everything I need. I am financially independent.

---

* Florence Scovel Shinn, *The Game of Life and How to Play It* (Marina del Rey, CA: DeVorss, 1925). (Masculine nouns and pronouns changed to feminine.)

DAY 13

What would give people more security as they age? Money was the No. 1 response, regardless of sex, age, income, race, or education. In fact, 40% put money at the top of their list—significantly more than those mentioning spouse (29%), children (12%), friends (5%), career/job (4%), or home (4%).

MARK CLEMENTS*

We're all doing better jobs with our money than we think. I've never known a woman who wasn't terrific with some aspect of money: saving it; buying cheaply and getting the best bargains; securing the cash for clothes, jewelry, or helping others; making money; investing it; giving it away; or even the inefficient method of finding others to give us what we want. However, few indeed have solved all the problems, or considered all the joys, of money.

AFFIRMATION

I plan for what I need.

---

* Mark Clements, "What We Say About Aging," *Parade Magazine,* December 12, 1993.

Positive thinking is realistic thinking. It always sees the negative, but it doesn't dwell on the negative and nurture it, letting it dominate the mind. It keeps the negative in proper size, and grows the positive big.

NORMAN VINCENT PEALE[*]

AFFIRMATION

In each situation I take all things into account but stay focused on the positive.

---

[*] Norman Vincent Peale, "Find Power in the Positive," *Plus,* April 1994.

DAY 15

Making one's own choices about the future is crucial for well-being.... Women do give up something when they take control of their own destinies—they give up the security of being dependent.... When you make your own decisions, you give up the right to be a victim, since you can't blame others for your life if it is one you have chosen.

GRACE BARUCH, ROSALIND BARNETT, AND CARYL RIVERS[*]

Because true power comes from within, we must nurture ourselves and take the necessary time to find out who we are. Most likely, our exploration of the self will lead to more spiritual knowledge and understanding.

AFFIRMATION

I can make financial decisions in my own best interests.

---

[*] Grace Baruch, Rosalind Barnett, and Caryl Rivers, *Life Prints: New Patterns of Love and Work for Today's Women* (New York: McGraw-Hill, 1983).

DAY 16

"I just see a mountain in front of me, and its name is Money."

Now, money is a very peculiar substance. It doesn't behave according to the laws of physics. Any amount you don't have—whether it's $5,000 or $500,000—will appear to be a mountain. Almost any amount you do have will not appear to be enough to pay next month's bills!...Being poor is one of the best excuses not to go for your dreams. It gets you much more sympathy than being fat. Nobody knows how to argue with poverty. We're all much too bamboozled by money in this society.

BARBARA SHER*

Working toward a big goal (financial independence) and embarking on a long journey both begin the same way: with first steps. We must break our big goal into manageable pieces. A beginning step may be saving five dollars a week and not even talking about "financial independence"—which may be a goal so large that we can't yet take it seriously. For clarifying our goals, Barbara Sher's helpful book suggests brainstorming, which she defines as gathering friends together to talk about your situation.

AFFIRMATION

I realize my dreams while improving my finances.

---

* Barbara Sher, *Wishcraft: How to Get What You Really Want* (Ballantine Books, 1979).

DAY 17

Think thoughts that make you happy.

LOUISE L. HAY*

If you can't monitor your own thoughts, now is the time to learn. To monitor your thoughts, you must first become aware of them. A simple exercise will suffice. Take paper, pen, and a timing device, find a quiet space alone, and for fifteen minutes simply note the thoughts that come. *Water the plants, Pick a mutual fund, Call Mother, I must lose ten pounds, Check out a bank loan.* Note the underlying categories of your thoughts. Do you beat yourself up? Take care of others and not yourself? Procrastinate? Make affirmations to change behaviors and thoughts that don't please you or don't fit your money goals.

Exercise: Just for today observe your thoughts and monitor how they affect your actions.

AFFIRMATION
I shed negative thought patterns that limit my abundance.

---

*Louise L. Hay, *You Can Heal Your Life* (Santa Monica, CA: Hay House, 1984).

Whether you are one of the winners in life...depends upon the choices you make at critical moments throughout your lifetime.

LOIS G. FORER*

AFFIRMATION

I gently review my past financial choices and plan for a bright future.

---

* Lois G. Forer, *What Every Woman Needs to Know Before (and After) She Gets Involved With Men and Money* (New York: Rawson Associates, 1993).

DAY 19

The point of power is always in the present moment. You are never stuck.

Maybe you need to take a walk. Or take a deep breath before beginning on one corner of the piled-up receipts. Maybe you need to make a list of how you spend money. Or take time right now to decide how you'll deal with a problem that's driving you crazy. Maybe you need to talk with a friend. Or be alone for a while.

Your power is in the present moment. How will you take it?

AFFIRMATION

Keeping my attention in the present moment helps me stay centered in my personal power.

---

* Louise L. Hay, *You Can Heal Your Life* (Santa Monica: Hay House, 1984).

DAY 20

How to begin? Let's be shameless. Be greedy. Pursue pleasure. Avoid pain. Wear and touch and eat and drink what we feel like. Tolerate other women's choices. Seek out the sex we want and fight fiercely against the sex we do not want. Choose our own causes. And once we break through and change the rules so our sense of our own beauty cannot be shaken, sing that beauty and dress it up and flaunt it and revel in it: In a sensual politics, female is beautiful.

NAOMI WOLF[*]

AFFIRMATION

I uncover my own sense of female beauty and it adds to my abundance.

---

[*] Naomi Wolf, *The Beauty Myth: How Images of Beauty Are Used Against Women* (New York: William Morrow, 1991).

DAY 21

But if you consciously determine to take on a new attitude of "I can't afford it because I have chosen to save ten percent, to pay the rent, to pay my bills, to give to others and to repay my debts" then you will begin to experience the serenity that accompanies financial responsibility and integrity.

MARY HUNT[*]

AFFIRMATIONS

- *I choose financial power and integrity.*
- *I choose to set limits on spending.*

[*] Mary Hunt, *The Best of the Cheapskate Monthly* (New York: St. Martin's Paperbacks, 1993).

DAY 22

Apply the notion of thoughts as things to the acquisition of wealth. If you picture yourself acquiring abundance, if you keep this vision in your mind regardless of the obstacles you encounter, and if you absolutely see it for yourself, then you will act on this image.

WAYNE W. DYER*

AFFIRMATION

Each and every day I picture myself acquiring abundance. As I see it, so it is.

---

* Wayne W. Dyer, *You'll See It When You Believe It: The Way to Your Personal Transformation* (New York: William Morrow, 1989).

DAY 23

We cannot solve life's problems except by solving them.

M. Scott Peck*

We have all known women who read book after self-improvement book while not self-improving. Many of us have been those women ourselves. Talking is a lot cheaper (and easier) than doing. At times we must simply jar ourselves out of inertia and deal with a dreaded problem or a difficult situation. Once when I moaned (for at least the hundredth time) over the masses of my writing papers I needed to put in order, my companion simply remarked, "Why don't you throw them all out?"

AFFIRMATION
Today I begin courageously facing my financial problems.

---

* M. Scott Peck, *The Road Less Traveled: A New Psychology of Love, Traditional Values and Spiritual Growth* (New York: Touchstone, 1978).

Help is as close as your own mind. The critical steps are being willing to ask and being willing to receive. As one contemporary saint expressed it, "No one is ever alone." Or as another said, "Your teacher is always with you, what varies is your willingness to listen."

JAMES FADIMAN*

Learning to hear and follow your internal voices can pay immense dividends. We have to pay attention to hear them, and they are easily lost in a busy routine. As a poet, I find that learning about my internal voices is an ongoing proposition. My best poetry is a gift. Words and phrases bubble up. I write and even rewrite them in my mind. When this happens I have two choices: I can grab paper and pen and get the words down. Or I can not listen or write, thinking I'll remember later. Invariably I'm left with regret that something good has passed me by—for, of course, all I can remember is that there was something I needed to remember.

AFFIRMATION

I am willing to cultivate the resources of my mind to achieve my personal and financial goals.

---

* James Fadiman, *Unlimit Your Life: Setting and Getting Goals* (Berkeley, CA: Celestial Arts, 1989).

DAY 25

To me, good health is more than just exercise and diet. It's really a point of view and a mental attitude you have about yourself. A strong, shapely body is of little use unless the person inside it greets each day with optimism.

ANGELA LANSBURY*

Good financial health is also more than savings and budgets. Basic attitudes of optimism or pessimism will help us toward, or hold us back from, our achievement of financial health, physical health, or any goal. We will be wise to reflect on our underlying attitude toward life. Deliberately cultivating our optimism pays immense dividends.

AFFIRMATIONS

- *I act as if I will succeed.*
- *Each and every day I become more optimistic about reaching my financial goals.*
- *I am a wise woman who is always safe and healthy, successful and rich, loving and loved.*

---

* Angela Lansbury, *Positive Moves: My Personal Plan for Fitness and Well-Being* (New York: Delacorte Press, 1990).

DAY 26

What I need to do has to happen in myself. Everything else is just a detour—falling in love, getting pregnant, whatever—just detours away from doing the real job, whatever that is.

That's what I have to learn to do: face things head on: no evasions, no detours, no easy ways out.

DOROTHY BRYANT*

A useful technique for me is to assess my abilities, my situation, and my possibilities within that situation, and then to imagine that five years have passed. Assuming my best efforts, am I pleased with where I find myself? If I am pleased then I go ahead with my work. If I am not, I reevaluate my desires (for example, how badly do I want money) and my situation, and begin to search for other options.

AFFIRMATION

I face my financial problems and allow self-discovery to become a key for change.

---

*Dorothy Bryant, *Ella Price's Journal* (Berkeley, CA: Ata Books, 1972).

DAY 27

I learned that our fear creates our own negativity. Negativity from other people as a thought form can certainly come into my field, but it's not going to harm me unless I allow it to. I can send it back to the person who sent it to me.

LYNN ANDREWS[*]

AFFIRMATION

Today I release the fear and negativity that obstruct my financial goals.

---

[*] Lynn Andrews, *The Woman of Wyrrd* (San Francisco: HarperSanFrancisco, 1990).

I reference money again because in the real world we need a certain amount of it every day. It gives us more options, and properly handled, it can enable us to broaden our sphere of influence and service. This is especially true if we remember that the real measure of our wealth is how much we would be worth if we lost all our money.

ZIG ZIEGLAR*

AFFIRMATION

I know the value of money and I plan to have what I need.

---

* Zig Zieglar, *Over The Top* (Nashville, TN: Thomas Nelson Publishers, 1994).

DAY 29

I have interviewed adults earning less than $5,000 a year who have successfully reconfigured their lives in order to be faithful to their highest inner values and spiritual needs. I also know individuals earning over $250,000 a year who feel unable to relinquish even a fragment of monetary security or social status to achieve a life they say they would prefer.

MARSHA SINETAR*

The prerequisites for spiritual growth are "positive self-value and learning resourcefulness," says Marsha Sinetar.

When we feel in conflict, we do not have our values sorted out at a deeper level. For example, I have sometimes needed to work very hard to achieve a goal, for only with its accomplishment could I discover that that goal was not what I really wanted.

We must learn that it is not money that keeps us from doing things, but ourselves who have not learned the lessons we need to learn.

AFFIRMATION

I define my level of prosperity according to my inner values and needs.

---

* Marsha Sinetar, *A Way Without Words: A Guide for Spiritually Emerging Adults* (Mahwah, NJ: Paulist Press, 1992).

DAY 30

Imagine that your thoughts are like drops of water....What kind of ocean are you creating?

LOUISE L. HAY*

I am still deeply impressed by the psychological study that talked of people's comfort zones and of how they strived to maintain them. People had quite clear notions of how much success (money, whatever) they should have, and *they kept themselves at the same level*. In other words, if they lost a lot, then they would win enough to stay in the same relative place. Conversely, the person who had received unexpected good luck and benefits would somehow devise how to lose these (in her unconscious view) undeserved goodies.

I came to realize that what needed changing (if I was to have the success I wanted) was my low self-esteem. To receive, I had to believe myself worthy of receiving.

AFFIRMATIONS

- *I am willing to have all the money, time, and fun that I want in my life.*
- *I notice those thoughts that restrict my prosperity and I lovingly release them.*

---

*Louise L. Hay, *The Power Within You* (Santa Monica, CA: Hay House, 1991).

Heed the New Commandments.... If you protect yourself, if you anticipate disaster, if you act on your own best judgment, if you are pleasant but firm, and if you discuss money in all your personal, family, and business relationships, you will have opportunities never before available to women.

LOIS G. FORER*

AFFIRMATION

I learn these new prosperity guidelines and act on them.

---

* Lois G. Forer, *What Every Woman Needs to Know Before (and After) She Gets Involved With Men and Money* (New York: Rawson Associates, 1993).

DAY 32

This view of work as temporary or as only play often prevents women from achieving a feeling of "getting someplace"—that is, building up for themselves a progressive sense of accomplishment, financial security, and real competency.... This can be a significant aspect of anyone's self-esteem.

ELIZABETH FRIAR WILLIAMS*

Learning our own worth is extremely important. Valuing what we do in monetary terms is necessary, not because we always plan to receive money, but because we need practice in setting worth on our time and competencies.

Exercise: Consider the concept of volunteer work, its meaning, and its financial implications in your life.

AFFIRMATION

I value my worth, work, and time.

---

* Elizabeth Friar Williams, *Notes of a Feminist Therapist* (New York: Dell, 1976).

DAY 33

The pitcher cries for water to carry and a person for work that is real.

MARGE PIERCY*

No one sits us down and says, "My dear, if you expect to be happy, find your Work." No one makes us understand that only work brings lasting respect in the world, self-esteem, purpose, and an organizing principle around which to order our lives. No one bothers to inform us that our Work may not pay us "diddly" yet may be the most joyful thing in our lives. No one tells us that finding our Work can be exasperating, disheartening, and that sometimes we can't even tell we've found it until we're halfway successful at it. Rarely is it written that our Work may be ephemeral, obscure, or its call so personal that ours are the only ears to hear it.

No one tells us that work and money and finances have their own rhythms and that we may have to make huge sacrifices for our Work or that, unexpectedly and after long labor, our Work may shower upon us the golden rain of money and the satisfaction of fulfilling our best potential.

AFFIRMATION

I open my heart to find my Work and my mind to figure out how to support it.

---

* Marge Piercy, "To be of use," *Circles on the Water* (1982). Quoted in Rosalie Maggio, ed., *The Beacon Book of Quotations by Women* (Boston: Beacon Press, 1992).

DAY 34

The manner in which we respond to negative criticism is a clue to the level of our self-esteem. If we harbor a feeling of inadequacy, negative criticism can wipe us out. Most of us carry with us too many internalized low-esteem messages from the past, negative things our parents or siblings or teachers or schoolday peers said to us.

ELISABETH RUEDY AND SUE NIRENBERG*

Elisabeth Ruedy is right when she tells us that our inner voices need new songs and new sentences to maneuver us through tough spots and to help keep us afloat through the day. She suggests that it is most productive to work daily with one affirmation that really speaks to us until it becomes comfortable and natural. *I am brilliant* is one she finds helps many of her clients with severe math anxiety. *I am comfortable dealing with money* is one I use.

AFFIRMATIONS

- *I receive appropriate financial criticism without loss of self-esteem.*
- *I am comfortable dealing with money.*

---

* Elisabeth Ruedy and Sue Nirenberg, *Where Do I Put The Decimal Point? How to Conquer Math Anxiety and Increase Your Facility with Numbers* (New York: Henry Holt, 1990).

DAY 35

You can be pleased with nothing when you are not pleased with yourself.

LADY MARY WORTLEY MONTAGU*

One reason for self-destructive behavior is that we don't know what else to do. What do you do when you're knocked off your path? Or you face a whole lot of rejections at once? When you have a fight with a loved one, or someone important to you puts you down?

We need easy and quick ways of "coming back to ourselves." One of the brightest women I know pulls weeds when she's upset. Another works with bonsai plants. Another meditates; one goes to a river cottage. One looks at art books, while another dives into music. I say, as honestly as I can, "Jo Ann is a loving child of the universe. She's doing the best she can with where she is, just as everyone is." And when I feel envious or resentful of others, I put *their* names in the affirmation. It's amazing how these affirmations lighten my load.

AFFIRMATIONS

- *When thrown off center I find healthy ways to renew myself.*
- *Each and every day I reclaim the power of providing for myself.*

---

* Quoted in Rosalie Maggio, ed., *The Beacon Book of Quotations by Women* (Boston: Beacon Press, 1992).

DAY 36

Good judgment comes when your logical and rational thoughts and ideas are supported by a gut reaction that the decision "feels" right, and you can live comfortably with the consequences of your action. Inner wisdom goes even farther because the decision not only feels right, but it also fits in with your values and beliefs. Something deep inside you can answer "Yes!"

BARBARA KILLINGER*

AFFIRMATION

I rely on my inner wisdom—the feelings, values, and beliefs within me—to create good financial judgment.

---

* Barbara Killinger, *Workaholics: The Respectable Addicts* (New York: Simon & Schuster, 1991).

DAY 37

How wrong it is for women to expect the man to build the world she wants rather than set out to create it herself. It is the source of woman's rebellions, her helplessness and dependency. I am setting out to create my own world, not to expect man to create it for me.

ANAÏS NIN[*]

AFFIRMATION

I take full responsibility for getting what I want.

[*] Anaïs Nin, *Diaries of Anaïs Nin, Vol. 1–7* (New York: Harcourt, Brace & Jovanovich, 1966–1980).

DAY 38

Having received little real nurturing yourself, you try to fill this unmet need vicariously by becoming a care-giver.

ROBIN NORWOOD*

If you received little nurturing, you can give yourself that gift.

AFFIRMATION

I nurture myself, financially and otherwise, in direct proportion to nurturing others.

---

* Robin Norwood, *Women Who Love Too Much: When You Keep Wishing and Hoping He'll Change* (New York: Pocket Books, 1985).

DAY 39

When you blame an outside force for any of your experiences of life you are literally giving away all your power and creating pain, paralysis and depression.

SUSAN JEFFERS[*]

Tying up our energy in nonproductive ways means we don't have it for attempting our financial goals.

AFFIRMATION

I take responsibility for my financial decisions and choices and cease to blame myself or others.

---

[*] Susan Jeffers, "Change What You Can Change," *Redbook,* February 1987.

DAY 40

[Getting rid of bad habits is] like getting rid of an alley cat. You don't have to kick it; just don't feed it.

GERALD G. MAY*

Addictions cost. Whatever form they take—alcohol, relationships, spending money—we want to be rid of them. The simplest solution I have found is to give no energy to the bad habit: I will kick no more alley cats.

Additionally, I expend no energy beating myself over the head for any lapses and backsliding. Instead, when I discover myself off my chosen path, without spending any excess energy, I simply return to the path. I call this technique the Path of Meditation and have learned to use it successfully in a wide variety of situations.

AFFIRMATION

I don't encourage my addictive behavior by obsessing about it. I simply redirect my attention to my chosen path.

---

* Gerald G. May, *Addiction & Grace* (San Francisco: Harper & Row, 1988).

DAY 41

Much of what I have to tell you about your body is common sense. You need to eat properly and get enough sleep. If you're working at an outside job to support yourself while writing, something's got to give. Don't let it be sleep. Give up your social life....For you to be successful, sacrifices must be made. It's better that they are made by others but failing that, you'll have to make them yourself.

RITA MAE BROWN*

We can't do our best job to make money or have optimal learning from an investment seminar if we don't have a healthy body and feel good physically. We must learn that taking care of ourselves physically is a top priority and decide to get on with it. Any course of action other than giving ourselves the care and feeding we require for optimal performance is stealing from ourselves. Allowing harm or putdowns to be directed against us, or putting ourselves down, are simply others forms of self-destructive behavior that we must not allow.

AFFIRMATIONS

• *I take care of my health and make appropriate sacrifices to achieve my financial goals.*

• *I create a healthy lifestyle and spend less than I earn.*

---

* Rita Mae Brown, *Starting From Scratch: A Different Kind of Writers' Manual* (New York: Bantam Books, 1988).

DAY 42

There is always a reason if you are feeling uncomfortable, hurt, worried, disappointed, angry, jealous, or otherwise emotionally upset. If the only reason you can come up with is another person and you cannot make them aware of your uncomfortable feeling and its origin—get away from that person.

JANET LEE MITCHELL*

It is interesting to consider that we have a duty to protect ourselves from negative people and to actively seek out those who are spiritually advanced. We must learn to notice our feelings and connect them with their sources—internal or external.

AFFIRMATION

I seek the companionship of those who help me to feel comfortable, uplifted, and supported in attaining my personal and financial goals.

---

* *How to Know God: The Yoga Aphorisms of Patanjali* (Hollywood, CA: Vedanta Press, 1962). Quoted in Janet Lee Mitchell, *Conscious Evolution.*

DAY 43

I also try to encourage women…to seek work that is financially reward-ing as well as personally gratifying…to stay in therapy until they have found a clear direction in terms of a career and until they know that they can perform and enjoy challenging work.

ELIZABETH FRIAR WILLIAMS*

All of my work, paid and unpaid, has financial implica-tions.

AFFIRMATION
I am willing to have a job that pays well and is personally satisfying.

* Elizabeth Friar Williams, *Notes of a Feminist Therapist* (New York: Dell, 1976).

DAY 44

Learn your lessons quickly, and move on.

EILEEN CADDY*

You can learn from every situation is an idea that crept up on me relentlessly. I didn't want to learn. I wanted all my problems solved—right now! But I discovered that wanting alone created no change. For example, merely wanting money did not affect the amount of money I had.

Rapid change for the better began as I adopted the motto, *Everything is a lesson.* I began asking myself: What does this situation have to teach me? What should I be learning? Blame, guilt, and procrastination slowly dropped away as I began learning from my difficulties. Many of my problems lessened—including the number and severity of my money concerns.

AFFIRMATION

I develop my financial skills by paying attention to the lessons I learn in my daily life and moving on.

---

* Eileen Caddy, *The Dawn of Change,* quoted in Susan Hayward, *A Guide for the Advanced Soul* (Crow's Nest, Australia: In-Tune Books, 1985).

DAY 45

I deserve to be prosperous and wealthy. (If money makes you feel guilty because you don't feel like you deserve it, then it is difficult to increase your income, because if you did you would just feel more guilty.)

PHIL LAUT*

This is why we really must examine our underlying belief systems. If somewhere inside our souls we have decided we are unworthy, unlovable, or unable, then as quickly as we build our accomplishments, the other side of us tears them down. For a house divided against itself, success—if possible—is a hundred times harder to achieve.

Affirmations help us unite our warring selves so we can work to make our dreams come true.

AFFIRMATION

I identify and eliminate any negative assumptions I have about money.

---

* Phil Laut, *Money Is My Friend* (New York: Ballantine Books, 1989).

DAY 46

You must mentally accept in the present what you want to literally happen in the future. Picturing it brings that acceptance much quicker...the picturing power of the mind turns your thinking from "I cannot have this" or "It will never happen to me" to hope, belief and finally to the mental acceptance that "It can happen to me" and "It will happen to me."

CATHERINE PONDER*

This "picturing," or visualization, is another form of affirmation. With visualization and with affirmation we are deliberately breaking apart our old limiting, negative mind sets.

AFFIRMATION

I picture what I want, and I allow myself to receive it.

---

* Catherine Ponder, *Open Your Mind to Receive* (Marina del Rey, CA: DeVorss, 1983).

DAY 47

When I talk about power with you, I am not talking about your having the sort of power over anyone that the king or the Church has. I am talking about personal power, your ability to make alive in the world your own dream.

LYNN ANDREWS[*]

Control is very important. Control doesn't mean ordering others around. It means feeling free to order your behavior in your own best interest. It means putting yourself at the center of your story and seizing your decision-making power, no matter how you choose to use that power.

AFFIRMATION

I give myself permission to reclaim my personal power and bring my financial dreams to life.

[*] Lynn Andrews, *The Woman of Wyrrd* (San Francisco: HarperSanFrancisco, 1990).

DAY 48

Maybe you grew up in what I call an "audience family": people who re-gard great achievements as the effortless products of a superior species, and can't see the long, slow, human process of development that leads up to them.

BARBARA SHER[*]

When I was young I never dreamed I could be a writer. I couldn't spell, no one could read my handwriting, and I knew I couldn't just spin out a story. Writers were magical creatures who sat down one day and wrote a book. I could never do that.

What I didn't know was that neither could they. Writing is both an art and a craft, and like many endeavors, it is partly a product of learning. When I saw how hard "real" writers worked, I began to understand that there were "how-to" methods to help me. I realized that behind any achievement is a long apprenticeship period. With this perspective, I gained the confidence to write.

AFFIRMATION

I accept the learning process that will help me become more financially savvy.

---

[*] Barbara Sher, *Wishcraft: How to Get What You Really Want* (New York: Ballantine Books, 1979).

Feminist: I myself have never been able to find precisely what feminism is. I only know that people call me a feminist whenever I express sentiments that differentiate me from a doormat.

REBECCA WEST, 1913[*]

Feminism to me is simply giving support to and receiving the support of women. The more we support one another, the more we can improve the financial possibilities for each of us.

AFFIRMATION

I support myself and all women in creating our financial empowerment.

---

[*] From Cheris Kramarae and Paula A. Treichler, *A Feminist Dictionary* (San Francisco: Thorsons, 1992).

DAY 50

...the hunger to create is not enough: One must in addition be inwardly free to pursue the creative task to completion.

SAMUEL J. WARNER*

Substitute "financial" task for "creative" task in this quote and we've named our problem: wanting financial security is not enough.

We must root out the self-defeating behavior that robs us of our freedom.

AFFIRMATION

I silence negative messages and behaviors and continue to pursue my monetary goals to completion.

---

* Samuel J. Warner, *Self-Realization and Self-Defeat* (New York: Grove Press, 1966).

DAY 51

These people were not rare or remarkable. But they were resilient. They often failed. But they always bounced back. Crisis, in fact, turns out to be the biggest confidence builder of all.

BARBARA BLOCK*

"Build your self-confidence," advises Judith Briles, author of *The Confidence Factor.* She defines confidence as the ability to pick yourself up and go on after a setback. She adds that "confidence comes from focusing on one's successes rather than one's shortcomings." (Which is exactly what affirmations help us do.) Quoting Temple University studies, Briles tells us that self-confident people get better jobs and make more money than the less confident. What better combination could we ask for than increasing our financial power and improving our relationship with ourselves at the same time?

AFFIRMATION

I allow adversity and setbacks to become a source of strength on the road toward prosperity.

---

* Barbara Block, "The Right Moves," *Gainesville Sun,* January 12, 1992.

DAY 52

Cecily went out into the garden. Her white border was looking spectacular; it had taken eight years to achieve. She had planned it...

JOANNA TROLLOPE*

The future can hold us hostage. We can live only for it, always getting ready to live—going to school, helping others, saving—and never living in the present. Or we can drift obliviously into a future we have not planned. Some of us do both at the same time.

Exercise: Take a sheet of paper and draw a line. Label one end *birth* and one end *death*. Fill in dates and your life's highlights. Marriage or partnership or love affairs, children, geographic moves, changes in jobs or careers, times you've been in school, financial highlights, buying a home, paying off a mortgage. Now look at your life all at once. Think into your future. What do you want to see written there? What garden are you planning now that you will view in eight years? In twenty?

AFFIRMATION

I achieve financial goals by considering past successes and planning for the future.

---

* Joanna Trollope, *A Village Affair* (New York: Harper & Row, 1989).

DAY 53

The stronger and more independent you are, the better your relationships will be.

STEVEN CARTER AND JULIA SOKOL.*

This is another way to say that the stronger and more independent you are, the more likely it is that all your relationships will be with other strong and independent people. Thaddeus Golas in *The Lazy Man's Guide to Enlightenment* says we attract people who vibrate at about the same level we do. Like attracts like. If we wish to have money and financial independence in our lives, then we should give thought to how we are attracting them to ourselves and to the ways we are being attracted to them.

How is your energy focused? According to Golas, when we try to raise others to our level, they resist and try to pull us down to their level. Because we attract what we project, we should embody in ourselves and in our actions those attributes we wish to find in others.

AFFIRMATION

I am a strong and independent woman focusing on achieving my financial goals and attracting like-minded people.

---

* Steven Carter and Julia Sokol, *What Smart Women Know* (New York: Dell, 1990).

DAY 54

The starting point in changing your life from financial reverses to an experience of abundance is the realization that you can change your life by altering your thoughts. You begin by taking responsibility for your own life.

ERIC BUTTERWORTH*

One meditation says: *Do everything for yourself.* The next meditation may say: *Do everything for others.* Should you follow your head or your heart? Use your focused consciousness or your diffuse consciousness?

Irene Claremont de Castillejo (*Knowing Woman: A Feminine Psychology*) says we all use focused consciousness in the everyday world all the time. However, Castillejo reminds us, focused is not the only kind of consciousness for "most children are born with, and many women retain, a diffuse awareness of the wholeness of nature, where everything is linked with everything else." Castillejo tells us to broaden our thinking, remembering that when we are in one consciousness "the other seems such nonsense that we tend to repudiate it wholly...I offend my head or I offend my heart."

AFFIRMATION

I create thoughts of prosperity and my reality follows.

---

* Eric Butterworth, *Spiritual Economics: The Prosperity Process* (Unity Village, MO: Unity School of Christianity, 1983).

...*true power does not have any more to do with the size of your office, the color of your luggage, or the lettering on your business card than it does with the size of your breasts, the grades your children make in school, or the flavor of your potato salad. True power has everything to do with knowing who you are and being it, knowing that at any moment you could lose any or all of the things named above.*

LEE MORICAL*

AFFIRMATION

Whatever I do brings me a strong sense of who I am and the opportunity to achieve true power through being myself.

---

* Lee Morical, *Where's My Happy Ending? Women and the Myth of Having It All* (Reading, MA: Addison-Wesley, 1984).

DAY 56

Since there is no way to avoid getting angry, we must learn to use anger to achieve our goals.

JOHN MUSGRAVE*

I've tried paying $10 to charity every time I get angry (I hate to *have to* spend money) and am doing Doris Helmering's exercise of saying "Nobody needs to get that angry," three thousand times a day for two months. I'm also studying the Dalai Lama's *A Policy of Kindness,* in which he urges compassion for all. And I'm working within my anger by visualizing it as energy I can transform to help me. John Musgrave suggests we visualize ourselves using our anger to squeeze an orange. Then we drink the juice, now imagining our anger as a source of positive energy.

AFFIRMATION

I harness the force behind my anger and direct it toward my financial solutions.

---

*John Musgrave, quoted in "Temper, Temper" by Frank Mixson, *Entrepreneurial Woman,* May/June 1990.

DAY 57

Self-awareness is the road to conscious choice in our behavior. If I am aware I am angry, I can choose to shout or write or take political action. If I am aware I am sad, I can find someone to talk to who will let me cry, or go jogging as a release. But if these feelings are not in my awareness, they take control of me, and I am in a state of confusion or anxiety.

NATALIE ROGERS[*]

AFFIRMATION

I use awareness and choice as keys to my successful financial behavior.

[*] Natalie Rogers, *Emerging Woman: A Decade of Midlife Transitions* (Point Reyes, CA: Personal Press, 1980).

DAY 58

Try to come to grips with the internal voices that sabotage the pursuing of our desires.

LUISE EICHENBAUM*

It's easy for us to tell ourselves we've done everything wrong, wasted all our chances, made too many mistakes, and it's too late anyway. We aren't worth it and our dreams mean nothing.

When you catch the voices in your head saying things like this, grab paper and pen and begin writing down what they say. If you can give them names, all the better. If not, just get busy making affirmations to counteract the negative voices. Every night before you sleep say, "I love you, ——— ." Use your name. This "I love you" is to make up for all the times you didn't hear it when you needed to.

AFFIRMATION

I continue to unburden myself from negative internal voices.

* Luise Eichenbaum, *Between Women: Love, Envy and Competition in Women's Friendship* (New York: Viking, 1988).

DAY 59

A lack of money merely mirrors the energy blocks within ourselves.

SHAKTI GAWAIN*

"Energy blocks" are ways we hold ourselves back. Energy blocks happen when we don't clean up old injuries or let go of negative emotions. When we are open to the universe, according to Shakti Gawain, we are open channels for abundance: "the more you are willing to trust yourself, and take the risks to follow your inner guidance, the more money you will have. The universe will pay you to be yourself and do what you really love!"

AFFIRMATIONS
- *I have no energy blocks about money.*
- *I allow myself to be an open channel for universal abundance.*

---

* Shakti Gawain, *Living In the Light* (San Rafael, CA: Whatever Publishing, 1986).

DAY 60

The battle of the sexes has no place between the balance sheets. In today's economy it's no longer possible for one sex to be the guardian of all financial knowledge while the other keeps love and home fires burning. We should all be equally conversant in the language of money.

VICTORIA FELTON-COLLINS*

Little tests the equality of a marriage like the generation and distribution of money. There are always differences of opinion—a thousand ways to spend or save money, use leisure time, set financial goals, or work together. What matters is how you and your partner settle your financial differences.

Exercise: Today pay full attention to how financial decisions are made in your relationship—who makes them, and how you feel about it.

AFFIRMATION

I do not make another financial opinion more important than my own.

---

*Victoria Felton-Collins, *Couples and Money: Why Money Interferes With Love and What to Do About It* (New York: Bantam Books, 1990).

DAY 61

The universe is a big dream machine, churning out dreams and trans-forming them into reality, and our own dreams are inextricably woven into the overall scheme of things.

DEEPAK CHOPRA*

Exercise: Examine and let go of the ways you hold yourself back from doing what you need and want to do.

AFFIRMATION

The universe holds a place for all my dreams and I have the courage to keep them alive.

---

* Deepak Chopra, *Creating Affluence: Wealth Consciousness in the Field of All Possibilities* (San Rafael, CA: New World Library, 1993).

DAY 62

It is essential to understand that there is a vast difference between being *inadequate and* feeling *inadequate.*

YVONNE KAYE*

Recently I watched a video of myself giving a speech and gained a lot of hope. On the video I was in control, projecting that I knew what I was talking about. My intense fear, shyness, and self-consciousness did not show. Hard work and practice on the speech had paid off although I had been extremely nervous.

Right then I decided to learn the lesson from the video: There was no correlation between what I felt and how I actually performed. And when I looked at my life overall, I was actually doing better in many areas (money goals, financial dealings) than I gave myself credit for.

AFFIRMATIONS

- *I act as if I will succeed in spite of my doubts.*
- *I give myself credit for my financial achievements.*

---

* Yvonne Kaye, *Credit, Cash and Co-Dependency* (Deerfield Beech, FL: Health Communications, 1991).

Five steps to making luck good: Find the action; Take measured risks; Learn when to bail out; Juggle a few different ventures; and Remember that life is unfair.

MAX GUNTHER*

AFFIRMATIONS

- *I foster good financial luck through action, risk, discernment, and diversity in my life.*

- *I am a lucky woman.*

---

* Max Gunther, *How to Get Lucky* (New York: Stein & Day, 1986).

DAY 64

In the world to come, each of us will be called to account for all the good things God put on earth which we refused to enjoy.

TALMUD*

There are many ways of being poor. Poor is having no friends. Poor is never seeing the sunlight. Poor is having financial resources and *feeling* poor.

AFFIRMATION

I pursue prosperity in its widest sense while being happy with what I have and where I am.

---

* Talmud, quoted in Harold Kushner's *When All You've Ever Wanted Isn't Enough: The Search for a Life That Matters* (New York: Pocket Books, 1986).

DAY 65

The will works to organize all available information and resources with the purpose of making decisions and creating behavior. Without the person's ability to will, there is no turning-point decision.... The will varies in strength, ability, and flexibility.

DONNA F. LAMAR[*]

When I can't do something or can't progress toward a goal, I've learned there is always a reason. That reason may be hidden from me. Many times I'm working toward the wrong goal. Or I may be resisting doing what is in my own best interest. Money decisions and financial goals are no different—if your will isn't working, find out why. If your resistance is working too well, find out what you're resisting—and why!

AFFIRMATION

Day by day I develop my will and lessen my resistance to having financial success.

---

[*] Donna F. LaMar, *Transcending Turmoil: Survivors of Dysfunctional Families* (New York: Plenum Press, 1992).

DAY 66

Specific negatives are the favorite negative ideas that people use to limit themselves. Whenever you feel depressed, write down all of your thoughts.

PHIL LAUT*

By writing the reasons down, you can identify the causes of your ordinary depression. (There is help for clinical depression and you should seek it if you need it.) The next time you feel depressed, set a timer for fifteen minutes, try to feel as depressed as you can, and write down every thought. Look over your list and you'll probably wonder why you aren't more depressed. Now, take the negative thoughts, invert them into affirmations, and begin writing the affirmations. If you are depressed over money, try working with one of the affirmations in this book.

AFFIRMATION

I notice and release the negative ideas that limit my financial gains.

---

* Phil Laut, *Money Is My Friend* (New York: Ballantine Books, 1989).

The message of our subjects' lives is that no one pattern fits all women, no one lifeprint guarantees well-being, and no one path leads inevitably to misery. Each pattern has its own clusters of joys and problems.

GRACE BARUCH, ROSALIND BARNETT,
AND CARYL RIVERS*

AFFIRMATION

I pay attention to my money pattern, aligning it with my financial goals.

---

* Grace Baruch, Rosalind Barnett, and Caryl Rivers, *Life-Prints: New Patterns of Life and Work for Today's Women* (New York: McGraw-Hill, 1983).

DAY 68

If something goes right, don't argue. Or to put it another way: when good luck pulls you sideways, let go.

MAX GUNTHER[*]

To be able to recognize when things are going right, we must be able to accept our right to have good luck happen to us.

AFFIRMATION

I am a lucky person who gets luckier and luckier.

---

[*] Max Gunther, *The Luck Factor* (New York: Macmillan, 1977).

DAY 69

The ancient Tao of living masters considered love, food and exercise the three columns supporting a woman's life. Longevity depended on the strength of these pillars.

JOLAN CHANG*

AFFIRMATION

I increase my longevity and prosperity through love, healthy food, and exercise.

---

* Jolan Chang, *The Tao of Love and Sex* (New York: Dutton, 1977). (Masculine pronoun changed to feminine.)

DAY 70

Contrary to popular belief, we workaholics are not women who are constantly doing something. We are often too busy and overworked, so that many times we just collapse into a morass of procrastination.

ANNE WILSON SCHAEF[*]

Turtling is the coping mechanism for burnout that I devised long before I knew about workaholics. To turtle, I take one problem, one concern, one behavior, or one goal and each day I simply do a little bit of work on it. Next day I do (or don't do, if I'm breaking a habit) a little more and the following day, still more. By recognizing these are long-term propositions, I escape the pressure of expecting an immediate change. With turtling as a means to my chosen ends, I hang in there, persevering and persevering.

AFFIRMATION

I work toward my financial goals a little bit each day, one day at a time.

---

[*] Anne Wilson Schaef, *Meditations For Women Who Do Too Much* (San Francisco: Harper & Row, 1990).

A workaholic is a person who gradually becomes emotionally crippled and addicted to control and power in a compulsive drive to gain approval and success....Workaholics cannot not work without becoming anxious.

BARBARA KILLINGER*

AFFIRMATION

I enjoy my work and know how to create a balanced life.

* Barbara Killinger, *Workaholics: The Respectable Addicts* (New York: Simon & Schuster, 1991).

DAY 72

I'm sick and tired of being sick and tired.

FANNY LOU HAMER, WOMAN'S RIGHTS ACTIVIST*

These are the words of someone ready to make a change. This is what I said when I got dead tired of being poor. When I could say, "I don't know what's in front of me, but I know what's here. *Anything* is better than this."

When we have resolved in our hearts that we need change, we eliminate ambivalence and become focused. Our task then becomes one of tactics—what is the best way to bring this change about?

AFFIRMATION

I call on my deepest and fullest resources to bring about the financial change I want.

---

* Quoted in Bill Clinton's Democratic nomination acceptance speech, 1992.

The immense success of our life is…in such common things that nothing can touch it. That is, if one enjoys a bus ride to Richmond, sitting on the Green smoking, taking the letters out of the box, combing Grizzle, making an ice, opening a letter, sitting down after dinner, side by side… well, what can trouble this happiness? And every day is necessarily full of it.

VIRGINIA WOOLF*

AFFIRMATION

I am open to the beauty and joy of all of life's abundance.

---

* Virginia Woolf, *A Moment's Liberty: The Shorter Diary* (San Diego: Harcourt Brace Jovanovich, 1984).

DAY 74

We are complaining about the ants at the picnic when the bears are eating our children.

BLAISE PASCAL[*]

We often divert ourselves with the trivial when something serious hangs over our heads—the woman doesn't check out the lump in her breast because she's too busy to take time off. The woman keeps a huge balance in her savings account instead of enjoying life or better investing her money. The woman has completed manuscripts sitting in her office while she reads yet another research book. Some of us even choose addictions as diversions.

AFFIRMATION

I take control of my time and life by focusing on my true priorities.

---

[*] Quoted in J. Keith Miller, *Compelled To Control: Why Relationships Break Down and What Makes Them Well* (Deerfield Beach, FL: Health Communications, 1992).

The more expansive your thoughts, the more expansive the reality you create.

SANAYA ROMAN*

AFFIRMATION

I open my mind to positive and expansive financial possibilities.

---

* Sanaya Roman, *Spiritual Growth: Being Your Higher Self* (Tiburon, CA: H. J. Kramer, 1989).

DAY 76

Affirmations are like planting seeds in the ground. When you put a seed in the ground, you don't get a full-grown plant the next day. We need to be patient during the growing season.

LOUISE L. HAY*

Change comes as we continue to say affirmations. We will release what we don't want. Or we will be ready ourselves to accept whatever change we want. Or our affirmations will open unexpected new avenues for us. We may have a brilliant brainstorm, or a friend may call with a suggestion, or the exact way to solve a money problem may fall into our hands. The point is, if you don't give up on affirmations, one way or another you will be led to the next step that will help you.

It is important to get the *form* of your affirmation down correctly. For example, when I finally learned enough to stop saying, "I am now happily married to *Tom*," (which I wasn't) and begin saying, "I am now in a happy relationship," I did eventually find myself in a happy marriage (but not to *Tom*).

AFFIRMATION

I enthusiastically expect my affirmations to work and I am patient in the process.

---

* Louise L. Hay, *The Power Within You* (Santa Monica, CA: Hay House, 1991).

LEARNING TO MANAGE
YOUR MONEY

Management involves planning, setting goals, acting on your plans, and keeping track of the actions. We use management to get what we want.

And how do we know what we want?

Find paper, pen, and a quiet place. Bring your mind to a space where you have unlimited time, talent, money, ability, self-confidence, support from your family, whatever you need. Now list a hundred things you would do and have and be. Don't lift your pen from the paper. Don't censor, write. And write and write. Play this game and you will learn some surprising results.

A friend who took a money course six years ago says she has now fulfilled most of her financial goals. She states that the degree to which you finish your hundred item list is the degree to which you will be prosperous. That is, if you only list sixty-five items, then you will meet only sixty-five percent of your goals!

Your money goals will come from you. Management involves the practical tools you need to make your goals into reality. Use this section to begin your journey into money management. And if you're already managing well, use these ideas to sharpen your money tools and bring new areas under your control.

DAY 77

I suggest making goals for the long term. Look at where you'd like to be in two years and set goals that will help you get there. This will give you a structure for change, but with very little pressure. Major areas for goal-setting:

Diet	*Play*
Exercise	*Life purpose*
Social support	*Meditation*
Creative thinking	

O. CARL SIMONTON[*]

Exercise: Today purchase a notebook for goals or begin a goal file.

AFFIRMATION

I am a successful money manager.

---

[*] O. Carl Simonton, *The Healing Journey: Restoring Health and Harmony to Body, Mind, and Spirit* (New York: Bantam, 1992).

DAY 78

I have had many clients who felt they did not have enough money. In all cases, the overall solutions called for obtaining more income, cutting expenses, or a combination of both. I have given the same kinds of advice to those people who eventually got what they wanted as I did to those who did not.

ALAN B. UNGAR*

It behooves us to find out what is really important to us, to learn the difference between needs and desires. One method is to cut to the bone. For a month, question every expense. Spend no unnecessary cent; list and account for every penny you do spend.

AFFIRMATION

I eagerly assess my incoming and outgoing monies and create a workable budget.

---

* Alan B. Ungar, *Financial Self-Confidence for the Suddenly Single: A Woman's Guide* (Los Angeles: Lowell House, 1989).

DAY 79

"You three are looking at a very wealthy woman."

"Are you trying to tell us that, by saving ten percent of every paycheck, you've turned yourself into a millionaire?"

"Precisely," was the incredible response.

DAVID CHILTON*

If you can't stand budgets but you still want a shot at being rich, David Chilton's *The Wealthy Barber* has a message you may want to hear. Don't let the title turn you off; this folksy account of a wealthy barber sharing his secrets with three people (including a single woman) is quietly informative, provocative, and solidly based in financial realities. The point of *The Wealthy Barber* is to teach you to become financially independent.

Exercise: Plan how you will become financially independent.

AFFIRMATION
I build prosperity in my life through planning.

---

* David Chilton, *The Wealthy Barber* (Rocklin, CA: Prima Publishing, 1991). (Masculine nouns changed to feminine.)

DAY 80

Harness what has been called "the greatest mathematical discovery of all time"—compound growth—and begin saving early. Starting at age 22, put $2000 every year in an IRA that invests the money in a mutual fund designed to track the Standard & Poor's 500.... Leave the money alone until you retire. By age 65...these modest savings will reward you with the equivalent of $404,392 in today's dollars, even after taxes.

READER'S DIGEST*

AFFIRMATION
Learning ways to invest money is fun!

---

* *Reader's Digest*, April 1994.

DAY 81

The economical homemaker with only her "egg money" to spend and the family checkbook to balance belongs to the past....If you intend to enter the financial world at all—and if you earn or control any money—you must do two things: You must learn about money, recognize your feelings about it and relate them to reality. And...you must learn the rules of the game.

ANNE KOHN BLAU*

Over and over, my financially successful women friends tell me: Don't take your financial advice solely from anyone who stands to make money from buying or selling your property (real estate, stocks and bonds, any investments). A suggestion I like is to always interview three potential advisors—lawyers, accountants, brokers, insurance agents—before choosing one.

AFFIRMATION

When it comes to the financial world and making money I learn the rules of the game.

---

* Anne Kohn Blau, *The Sex of The Dollar* (New York: Simon & Schuster, 1988).

Without question, the number-one priority for midlife and older women right now is economic security. The poverty rate for women is about 65 percent higher for older women than for older men...25 percent of all women working now can expect to be poor in their old age.

MARY ROSE OAKAR, CONGRESSWOMAN*

AFFIRMATION

I begin now to plan for old age.

---

* Mary Rose Oakar, quoted in Jane Porcino's *Growing Older, Getting Better* (New York: Continuum, 1991).

DAY 83

Only the powerless live in a money culture and know nothing about money. Ignorance about money and power is not an effective means of acquiring, redefining, or redistributing them. A political, "sophisticated," or religious horror of money dangerously avoids the fact that, in a money culture, it is only money that buys the things that all people want—and deserve: life, health, food, land, hope, education, sexual pleasure, and some peace of mind.

PHYLLIS CHESLER AND EMILY JANE GOODMAN*

Once in my adult life I was totally at the mercy of the world: no money, no education, no property, no real work, no self esteem, no supportive circle of friends. I vowed then to get out of that powerless position and to stay out of it.

AFFIRMATION
In reclaiming my personal power I consciously begin educating myself about money.

---

* Phyllis Chesler and Emily Jane Goodman, *Women, Money and Power* (New York: Bantam Books, 1977).

DAY 84

Faked and fought over, hoarded, invested, and squandered, money is the fuel that keeps society moving.

PETER T. WHITE*

Money. Money. Money. *National Geographic* uses pictures to help me understand the meaning of money. I see strange old coins, the stock exchange, and a picture of Sheelah Ryan, the Florida lottery winner who has received over 750,000 letters asking for assistance. A bride exchanged for eleven pigs used as money is shown, as is a day's wage for a Roman soldier. This article on the fascinating history of money is worth a trip to the library.

AFFIRMATION

I give thought to what money really is and I consider ideas of barter.

*Peter T. White, "The Power of Money," *National Geographic*, January 1993.

DAY 85

As a Navajo tribal chairman has said, "Traditional Navajo values do not include poverty."

ROBERT H. WHITE[*]

Does poverty really build character? White explains how some people without power get it:

> The tribes in this book have succeeded in part because they hire the best technical and managerial help they can find or afford. Their leaders are keenly interested in creating jobs for their constituents but have no interest in setting up their people for failure just to satisfy a half-baked conception of "doing it themselves."

I wallowed along in poverty for years, embracing many half-baked notions about the integrity of struggling. Having money is more satisfying than clinging to those notions.

AFFIRMATION

I clarify my conceptions about money's power. I learn what money is and what money power can do for me.

---

[*] Robert H. White, *Tribal Assets: The Rebirth of Native America* (New York: Henry Holt, 1990).

DAY 86

A McCall's *survey reveals that most young women make no plans for their retirement. "This can be the costliest mistake they'll ever make," an expert warns.*

CHRISTOPHER HAYES[*]

"This is a wonderful book," I exclaim to a woman in my discussion group. An active single mother whose only son just graduated from college, she is also the newly elected president of our church. "Even if you're starting in your thirties, this book tells you exactly what you need to know and has easy action plans to tell you what to do." I hand her *Creating Your Own Future: A Woman's Guide to Retirement Planning.* "It's terrific." My friend is active in politics and the National Organization for Women, owns her own home, and knows quite a bit about money.

"I'll have to think about that sometime." Disinterest drips from every syllable and she puts the book down. Surprise renders me speechless.

AFFIRMATION
Now is the time for me to plan my retirement.

---

[*] Christopher Hayes, "Financial Security: What Every Woman Must Know," McCall's, October 1989.

The purpose of writing your [financial] goals is to convert your dreams into a workable set of realistic and achievable aims.

JUDITH MARTINDALE AND MARY MOSES[*]

Each woman will find her own way through the maze of life to her own level of financial independence and security. Luckily for women, new role models and creative ideas constantly appear. For example, Amy Dacyczyn combines staying at home to raise children with a high level of creative thrift to produce the *Tightwad Gazette,* a monthly pamphlet of helpful saving and financial hints.

AFFIRMATION

I create financial goals in order to make my dreams come true.

---

[*]Judith Martindale and Mary Moses, *Creating Your Own Future: A Woman's Guide to Retirement Planning* (Naperville, IL: Sourcebooks Trade, 1991).

DAY 88

Opportunity doesn't knock once. It's pounding on the door, tearing off the roof, and kicking in the windows all the time. It's a matter of perspective, of being willing and ready to see it.

JERROLD MUNDIS*

There are numerous ways to view opportunities. So often I've been pushed kicking and screaming into some of my best opportunities for making money and improving my life. Every door I wanted to open was closed—my *opportunity* consisted of taking the only door that would open.

Of any situation we can ask: What will this experience teach me? Do I reserve my strength now, or use it? Where is my opportunity in this situation?

AFFIRMATION

I recognize appropriate financial opportunities and make them work for me.

---

* Jerrold Mundis, *How to Get Out of Debt, Stay Out of Debt and Live Prosperously* (New York: Bantam Books, 1988).

DAY 89

Control starts with planning. Planning is bringing the future into the present so that you can do something about it now.

ALAN LAKEIN*

Exercise: Write a one-hundred item list of goals.

AFFIRMATION

As I begin financially planning my future I move away from fear and into possibility.

---

* Alan Lakein, *How to Get Control of Your Time and Your Life* (New York: Signet, 1973).

DAY 90

There are really three amounts you should decide upon: first, a yearly income you wish to earn now or in the future; second, the amount of money you wish to have saved in the near future; and third, the amount of money you would like to have as retirement income, whether you retire from active work or not. Write down these three amounts.

DENNIS KIMBRO*

Exercise: Today, for ten minutes, ponder your answers to these three questions.

AFFIRMATION

I open to the excitement of creating a solid financial future.

---

*Dennis Kimbro, *Think and Grow Rich: A Black Choice* (New York: Fawcett, Columbine, 1991).

DAY 91

Love your bills. It is essential that we stop worrying about money and stop resenting our bills.

LOUISE L. HAY[*]

Not long ago I sat down to write a series of checks that would add up to nearly $1,000. Before paying these bills, I deliberately adjusted my outlook. I decided to be grateful for the opportunity to write the checks and happy that I had the money. This was a joyous occasion. I would treat it with respect.

AFFIRMATION

I treat the exchange of money with respect, and what I send out returns two fold.

---

[*] Louise L. Hay, *You Can Heal Your Life* (Santa Monica: Hay House, 1984).

DAY 92

The first step in making a financial plan that will fit your new circumstances is figuring out what you have been spending. It always surprises me that most people don't know how much they spend.

MICHAEL STOLPER[*]

It seems such a simple idea: when your circumstances change, you need a new plan. You need to rethink where you are and what is going on in your life. This thinking can be quite revealing. Several years ago, I felt ragged, as if I wasn't accomplishing anything. I sat down and listed my daily and weekly tasks. Imagine my surprised relief when I discovered I had three full-time jobs! I immediately begin figuring how to reorganize and lighten up.

The same self-revelation can happen when you examine your spending habits. Go back through your checkbook and credit card bills for a year. Don't worry over a big one-time expense; expect that every year will contain one such expense. Armed with accurate information about your spending habits, you can make new plans to optimize your changed circumstances.

Exercise: Find out what you are spending and consider your overall financial plans.

AFFIRMATION

I spend less than I earn.

---

[*] Michael Stolper, *Wealth: An Owner's Manual: A Sensible, Steady, Sure Course to Becoming and Staying Rich* (New York: HarperBusiness, 1992).

DAY 93

When a man tells a woman not to worry about a subject she wants to discuss, whether it is money or property or family members, that is a clear sign of a problem. *It will not disappear simply because you are told not to worry about it.*

LOIS G. FORER[*]

AFFIRMATION
Only I can be responsible for my financial future and my well-being.

---

[*] Lois G. Forer, *What Every Woman Needs to Know Before (and After) She Gets Involved With Men and Money* (New York: Rawson Associates, 1993).

DAY 94

When I saw that I could go into a store, pick up an item, and say, "This will cost me three hours of life energy," I became much more conscious. Before, I'd just have bought it.

MARCIA MEYER[*]

AFFIRMATION

I evaluate all purchases based on the cost of my life energy.

[*] Marcia Meyer, quoted in Lisa Stone, "America on $16 a Day," *New Age Journal*, November/December 1990.

DAY 95

If I gave this [money management] course to Ben Franklin, he'd laugh me off the stage. It's just basic, universal wisdom that we've forgotten over the generations.

JOE DOMINGUEZ*

AFFIRMATIONS

- *My relationship with money is lifelong. I put effort into making it a good one.*
- *My partner and I create clear financial goals together and align our efforts to accomplish them.*

---

* Joe Dominguez, *Transforming Your Relationship With Money and Achieving Financial Independence: A Complete Audio Cassette/Workbook Course* (Seattle, WA: The New Road Map Foundation, 1986). See also: Joe Dominguez and Vicki Robin, *Your Money or Your Life* (New York: Viking/Penguin, 1992).

DAY 96

What can you do to improve your financial lot right now, in your present job, with your present skills? At a minimum: don't lose money. This is the first rule of personal finance. Women are often either more conservative than men, in which case they lose investment income, or they tend to be more speculative, in which case they lose the principal invested.

JOAN GERMAN-GRAPES*

AFFIRMATIONS

- *I am serious about improving my financial situation.*
- *I use money to make money.*

---

* Joan German-Grapes, *Ninety Days to Financial Fitness* (New York: Collier Books, 1993).

DAY 97

I wish that from the age of eighteen I had had a really knowledgeable attitude about money. My God! It determines the quality of your life. Women should become aware of money as a power. If you are a middle-aged woman and you haven't got a pension plan, you'd better start thinking. So much of your future is going to depend on economic resources.

FIFTY-SIX-YEAR-OLD WOMAN*

This quote says it all. We must contemplate our financial future. Will we live alone? Are we responsible for others? What exactly would happen if our partner died or left us?

Exercise: Explore the options of having your own saving, checking, and investment accounts and retirement plan.

AFFIRMATION

I educate myself about my financial position and I take steps to improve it.

---

* Gillie Beram and Caroline T. Chauncey, "Money Matters; The Economics of Aging for Women," *Ourselves Growing Older* (New York: Simon & Schuster, 1987).

DAY 98

Spending is the forbidden apple of the financial Garden of Eden, where all our troubles begin.

Spend too much and you fall into debt.

Fall into debt and you can't save.

Fail to save and you have nothing to invest.

With nothing invested, you're up the inflation tree.

STEVE CROWLEY*

AFFIRMATION

I can set limits on spending.

---

* Steve Crowley, *Money for Life* (New York: Simon & Schuster, 1991).

DAY 99

There are only four ways I know of to spend less and thereby free up more dollars to be saved: Make things last longer. Use smaller quantities. Buy cheaper. Use a cheaper substitute.

MARY HUNT[*]

AFFIRMATION

I become more and more creative in finding ways to spend less and save more.

[*] Mary Hunt, *The Best of the Cheapskate Monthly* (New York: St. Martin's Paperbacks, 1993).

DAY 100

Saving money on groceries depends on a consistent attitude toward shopping—every time you shop. It is essential that you enter the supermarket fully conscious and determined about what you will—or will not buy.

AMY DACYCZYN*

AFFIRMATIONS

- *I consistently save money on groceries.*
- *I learn how to eat better for less.*

---

* Amy Dacyczyn, "How Amy Dacyczyn Avoids Overspending at the Supermarket," *Bottom Line,* October 15, 1993.

DAY 101

How do you break the spending habit? The way you break any undesirable habit: you retrain yourself in manageable increments.

STEVE CROWLEY*

AFFIRMATION

Today I begin to break my bad spending habits.

---

* Steve Crowley, *Money for Life* (New York: Simon & Schuster, 1991).

Formula for success: Establish a believable goal and write it down… visualize yourself already accomplishing that goal…always maintain a positive attitude…don't give up, even when things are going wrong… work…work…work…work…work.

RICHARD DIGGS*

If I'm to fulfill my financial ambitions, times will come when I have to work and I don't want to. Usually I'm fine, but when I get stuck I 1) cut the job in smaller pieces, 2) ask if there's any part of it I can bring myself to do. (At this point I also give myself a pep talk, and if that doesn't work, I probe to discover any bribe I can offer myself), and 3) finally I realize that a wiser part of me knows I'm trying to do the wrong thing, or perhaps a job that's better left undone. Sometimes the task *is* finished and I don't know it!

Exercise: Let your goals sit in your mind. Ask yourself, "Is this something I'd get up at 5 o'clock in the morning to do?"

AFFIRMATION

I set and honor realistic goals for success.

---

* Richard Diggs, *Finding Your Ideal Job* (Homosassa, FL: Progressive Publications, 1988).

DAY 103

Every expenditure falls into one of two categories: essential or optional. Essential expenses are those items necessary for life:...Basic food. Basic clothing. Basic shelter. Basic transportation. Taxes. Insurance. Savings.

MARY HUNT*

AFFIRMATION

I know what my essential expenses are. And my optional ones.

---

* Mary Hunt, *The Best of the Cheapskate Monthly* (New York: St. Martin's Paperbacks, 1993).

DAY 104

If a woman believes it is immoral, greedy, or selfish to act in her own behalf in the marketplace, she may never be able to examine the fears that stand between her and financial success.

ANNETTE LIEBERMAN AND VICKI LINDNER*

Our beliefs shape our behavior. Our behavior shapes our life. Yet many times our beliefs, since they are below the level of consciousness, are not readily available to us and we may find ourselves acting on beliefs we don't know we have.

Exercise: Examine your beliefs about money until you know what they are. Decide to change those that don't serve you.

AFFIRMATION

I act on my own financial behalf.

---

* Annette Lieberman and Vicki Lindner, *Unbalanced Accounts: How Women Can Overcome Their Fear of Money* (New York: Penguin Books, 1987).

DAY 105

Money is a topic that activates shame for everyone.....When you are ashamed about money, no amount seems right...money is a whole lot more subjective and emotional than is commonly believed.

PHIL LAUT*

AFFIRMATION

I release all shame about having money. It's good for me to have money.

---

* Phil Laut, *Money Is My Friend* (New York: Ballantine Books, 1989).

DAY 106

A hang-up is the remembered effect of a real or imagined unpleasant previous experience that holds us back, blocks progress or interferes with the free flow of energy, ambition, interest, action and ideas.

MAYA PILKINGTON*

Hang-ups cause problems and get seriously in the way of our enjoyment of life. If we don't stop to analyze these blocks and figure out better ways to do things—and then actually take those steps—we can hold on to our financial hang-ups forever.

When you find yourself having the same old argument about money, or feeling that familiar guilt when you buy something for yourself, you could begin investigating ways to displace and defuse your hang-ups. *The Real-Life Aptitude Test* contains excellent material about dismantling hang-ups, complete with diagrams.

AFFIRMATION

I let go of financial hang-ups and I open to a free flow of monetary energy in my life.

---

* Maya Pilkington, *The Real-Life Aptitude Test* (New York: Pharos Books, 1987).

DAY 107

Money is an emotional as well as economic commodity.

JUDITH BROWN*

We all use money at times to make ourselves feel better. But by clearly separating emotional from economic needs, we can avoid paying too much for "dance lessons" when what needs addressing is our feeling of loneliness. Conversely, when our economic needs are dire we can take clear action, if we are not ashamed to ask for help well before we are desperate.

AFFIRMATION

I separate my emotional and economic needs in order to further my financial goals.

---

*Judith Brown, *A Second Start: A Widow's Guide to Financial Survival at a Time of Emotional Crisis* (New York: Simon & Schuster, 1986).

DAY 108

The more positive your attitude toward money, the greater will be your "wealth-potential," since the biggest threat to your success will be any inner feelings that conflict with your aims.

MAYA PILKINGTON*

AFFIRMATION

I am becoming more and more positive toward money and increasing my wealth potential.

---

* Maya Pilkington, *The Real-Life Aptitude Test* (New York: Pharos Books, 1987).

DAY 109

"What," men have asked distractedly from the beginning of time, "what on earth do women want?" I do not know that women, as women want anything in particular, but as human beings they want, my good men, exactly what you want yourselves: interesting occupation, reasonable freedom for their pleasures, and a sufficient emotional outlet.

DOROTHY L. SAYERS*

AFFIRMATION

I know what I want and I pursue it.

* Dorothy L. Sayers, *Are Women Human?* (Grand Rapids, MI: William B. Eerdmans Publishing, 1971).

DAY 110

So you never bothered to get a library card....You're missing out on the best bargain in town. Today's public libraries offer film shows, music workshops, antique exhibits, poetry readings, lectures, and more—all for free. Many offer computers for public use, albums and cassettes for loan, and holiday programs for children.

RODALE PRESS[*]

AFFIRMATION

I uncover the free resources available to me as part of my financial planning.

---

[*] *Cut Your Bills in Half* (Emmaus, PA: Rodale Press, 1989).

DAY 111

Learning how to learn is the ultimate employment security. If your job or occupation is eliminated, you simply choose another one and learn how to be the best you can be. That's why well-educated people who are in good health and willing to work rarely face chronic unemployment problems. They know how to learn. It's those without basic learning skills that face big-time problems in the new economy. As a Haitian proverb put it: "Ignorance doesn't kill you, but it makes you sweat a lot."

MICHAEL LEBOEUF[*]

Exercise: Evaluate your basic learning skills and make plans to add to them if you need to.

AFFIRMATION

I love to learn new things, especially about employment and money.

[*] Michael LeBoeuf, *Fast Forward* (New York: G. P. Putnam's, 1993).

DAY 112

Living debt-free should be your ultimate goal. At that point, you're paying for the goods and services themselves, and not for the use of the money. The only thing debt does is make us pay more for what we're buying. Living debt-free, you're no longer paying an extra 5 or 10 percent or more—sometimes a great deal more—for everything you buy.

STEVE CROWLEY*

AFFIRMATION

I am becoming more and more debt free.

---

* Steve Crowley, *Money for Life* (New York: Simon & Schuster, 1991).

DAY 113

As a widow, having sufficient income and investing wisely are of paramount importance to you. Of equal importance is insurance which protects the assets you have already acquired. Most people think of life insurance when they hear the word "insurance," but also to be considered are: health, long-term care, disability, auto, household and liability insurance.

ALEXANDRA ARMSTRONG AND MARY R. DONAHUE[*]

The first goal of health insurance is risk control, according to Donald Korn in *Your Money or Your Life.* "You want to avoid the risks of a huge medical bill that will cost you everything you own."

AFFIRMATION

I am persistent and creative in getting the insurance coverage I need.

---

[*] Alexandra Armstrong and Mary R. Donahue, *On Your Own: A Widow's Passage to Emotional and Financial Well-Being* (Dearborn, MI: Financial Publishing, 1993).

DAY 114

It's true that you have choices when you have money. And if you do, you can invest in boats or clothes...or you can say, "I'm going to invest in myself."

TOMIMA EDMARK, INVENTOR OF TOPSYTAIL[*]

AFFIRMATION

I invest in myself and my future.

---

[*] Judie Glave, "TopsyTail Turns the Right Side Up for Inventor," The Associated Press, February 13, 1994.

DAY 115

I've always thought that people choose partners for the wrong reasons; they both like French movies or Swiss chocolate. They don't spend enough time focusing on the issues that mean the most to us, such as money.

VALERIE FRIEDMAN, FINANCIAL PLANNER*

The time to talk about money (or anything else) is as soon as you discover there are problems. An approach that helps me is illustrated by card six of the tarot, *"the Lovers."* This card shows two lovers, naked, neither hiding anything, while above them is a third presence, the "we-ness" of their relationship. This "we-ness" is where I focus attention during financial discussion, and I remind my partner to focus there also.

AFFIRMATION

I'm willing to do the work that it takes to have the relationship I want, and the finances I need.

DAY 116

The average age at which a woman is widowed is 56; only 6 percent of women 70 and older are married.

JUDITH MARTINDALE AND MARY MOSES*

Even if you're only thirty, and especially if you're older, probably one of the best things you could do for your financial self would be to study Judith Martindale and Mary Moses's book, *Creating Your Own Future: A Woman's Guide to Retirement Planning.* This book has a great deal of good information, with lists that gently guide you through the mazes of social security, pensions, wills, and medical insurance, among other things.

AFFIRMATION

I prepare now for old age and retirement.

---

* Judith Martindale and Mary Moses, *Creating Your Own Future: A Woman's Guide to Retirement Planning* (Naperville, IL: Sourcebooks Trade, 1991).

DAY 117

I have always believed that teamwork has been our greatest economic asset.

AMY DACYCZYN*

What do you do when your partner is a spender and you are a saver? Or what if the opposite is true?

Lee Morical, author of *Where's My Happy Ending?: Women and the Myth of Having It All,* using the image of dirty towels left on the bathroom floor, gives us a problem-solving method with five choices that we can apply to many situations:

1. Teach everyone to pick up her or his own things. (Get others to cooperate and help you.)

2. Pick them up yourself. (Consider this cost to you; that is, what are you giving up to do it?)

3. Hire someone to pick them up. (Go outside to get what you can't get at home.)

4. Let them stay on the floor. (Do nothing; this is also a method of Tough Love: letting others feel the consequences of their behavior; this will not make you popular.)

5. Yell at others to pick them up. (Waste your life.)

AFFIRMATION

I seek to create teamwork and mutual goals in all my economic partnerships.

---

* Amy Dacyczyn, *Tightwad Gazette,* February 1992.

119

DAY 118

Men and women deal with money differently. They perceive it, use it, speak about it, and live with it in surprisingly diverse ways. Of course, it would be ridiculous (and wrong) to even suggest "all men" or "all women" are exactly the same. Nevertheless, I have noticed that the sexes diverge in three areas: training, experience, and attitude.

VICTORIA FELTON-COLLINS*

Raised within the stereotypical male-as-provider and female-as-nurturer model, I have had to make many adjustments. A big one is accepting financial responsibility for myself, now and in the future. I've learned to question bargains I make with partners and to clarify them. For example, these savings I'm working so hard to accumulate—whose are they? This housework and relationship adjustment I do—is it valued? What will my partner and I live on when we're old? What will I live on if my partner isn't around?

AFFIRMATION

I accept financial responsibility for myself. I clarify my money goals and put them into operation.

---

* Victoria Felton-Collins, *Couples and Money: Why Money Interferes With Love and What to Do About It* (New York: Bantam Books, 1990).

DAY 119

You do it [figure your net worth] by putting together a personal balance sheet that summarizes what you own and what you owe.

MARGUERITE T. SMITH*

Exercise: Figure your net worth:

1. List by name *everything* you own, including checking and savings accounts, CDs, Keoghs, jewelry, cash, value life insurance, house, and so forth.

2. Next to every asset, write down its current market value (if you sold it now, how much money would it bring?) For life insurance, note the cash value.

3. Add them up. These are your assets.

4. On another page, list the names of your creditors, including credit cards, charge accounts, home mortgage, and any loans for cars, college, and investments.

5. Next to each creditor's name, write the amount you still owe.

6. Add up your liabilities.

7. Subtract liabilities from assets to arrive at your net worth.

AFFIRMATION

I know my assets, my liabilities, and my net worth.

---

* Marguerite T. Smith, "How to Start Controlling Your Spending," *Money Guide to Personal Finance,* Spring 1989.

If you're out of money, out of a job, and you just got evicted from your apartment, the chances are pretty good that you're "in survival," or "in your first chakra." This is to say that most or all of your psychic attention is being directed to maintaining the basics of life.

AMY WALLACE AND BILL HENKIN*

Exercise: Carefully consider your means of survival, and develop a bottom-line contingency plan.

AFFIRMATION

Today I move beyond "just surviving" and begin saving money.

---

* Amy Wallace and Bill Henkin, *The Psychic Healing Book* (Berkeley, CA: Wingbow Press, 1978).

When you seek a job bear in mind these four principles:
   1. You are working for money.
   2. Your work is not an act of charity.
   3. Your work is not a hobby.
   4. As an employee you have rights.

LOIS G. FORER*

AFFIRMATION

I own my power in the workplace and protect my own interests.

---

* Lois G. Forer, *What Every Woman Needs to Know Before (and After) She Gets Involved With Men and Money* (New York: Rawson Associates, 1993).

There is no magic formula or secret system to finding a job. New jobs are created every day. According to the Bureau of Labor Statistics almost one worker in five enters or returns to an occupation he or she did not work in 12 months earlier. Your chances of finding employment are good if you conduct your campaign in a systematic, businesslike way.

J. ROBERT CONNOR[*]

AFFIRMATION

I realize that getting a job is a job and I work at it like any other job.

---

[*] J. Robert Connor, *Cracking the Over-50 Job Market* (New York: Penguin, 1992).

DAY 123

A master plan for removing hidden barriers: Examine your script and make the necessary changes. Stop blaming others for your problems. Solicit feedback on the actions you take. Stop denying the existence of problems. Make positive changes in your life. Modify or leave relationships that divert you from your career goals. Get appropriate help from your organization. Visualize self-enhancing behavior. Make happiness your goal.

ANDREW J. DUBRIN[*]

AFFIRMATION

I can change my behavior, even when part of my mind doesn't want to.

---

[*] Andrew J. DuBrin, *Your Own Worst Enemy: How to Overcome Career Self-Sabotage* (New York: AMACOM, 1993).

DAY 124

If you want to take the true measure of someone, observe how she handles sex, time, and money.

JACOB NEEDLEMAN*

Think about this: Sex. Time. Money.
Time. Money. Sex. Money. Sex. Time.
Money. Time. Sex. Money. Money. Money.

Does your mind hit on money and skitter off? Money. Money. Money. To help you focus, imagine your largest closet is filled, top to bottom, with greenbacks of a large denomination. This money is a gift to you from an unknown benefactress who has also given you legal papers proving she gave it to you.

Moneymoneymoneymoneymoneymoneymoneymoney

AFFIRMATION

Today I consider what I would do with lots and lots and lots of money.

---

*Jacob Needleman, *Money and the Meaning of Life* (New York: Doubleday, 1991). (Masculine pronoun changed to feminine.)

DAY 125

Common ways debt is incurred: Taking a cash advance on a credit card. Purchasing fuel with a gasoline card. Paying for a meal with a credit card. Buying mail order using a credit card. Failing to pay the rent on time (you owe it, so a debt is created). Any contract requiring a signature and installment payments.

MARY HUNT*

AFFIRMATION

I am superconscious of debt and how I become and remain debt free.

---

* Mary Hunt, *The Best of the Cheapskate Monthly* (New York: St. Martin's Paperbacks, 1993).

DAY 126

In the beginning, saving is all give and little get.

LANI LUCIANO*

Lani Luciano gives seven suggestions to help us get serious about saving. (These ideas work best if you're holding a paying job.) We've heard them before, but repetition helps make them stick in our minds during the tough times: pay in cash; make bigger down payments; if you own a home, use a home-equity loan to consolidate high-interest debts; eliminate one big expense a year; don't pay for financial services you can get for free; save your next raise; and take advantage of your company's saving plan.

Saving money is as individual as we are; we have to find methods that work for us.

AFFIRMATION
I find good methods for saving money and I use them.

---

* Lani Luciano, "How to Start Controlling Your Spending," *Money Guide to Personal Finance,* Spring 1989.

There are three ways to convert your negative cash flow to positive: 1) decrease expenses; 2) increase income; and 3) sell assets to raise cash to pay off debt.

MARY HUNT[*]

AFFIRMATION

I accept the responsibility of converting negative cash flow to positive.

---

[*] Mary Hunt, *The Best of the Cheapskate Monthly* (New York: St. Martin's Paperbacks, 1993).

DAY 128

I shall never balk at the name or the color, if it is delicious and appetizing. Pleasure is one of the principal kinds of profit.

MONTAIGNE[*]

That old Protestant ethic keeps tripping us up. We think the only way to advance is work, work, work. Think now of another view. "Boredom is unearned leisure," says a friend. If you've earned your "profit" of leisure, take it. Don't be so hard on yourself. If you haven't earned your leisure-profit, make sure you do!

AFFIRMATION

I include pleasure among my assets and know when I have earned it.

---

[*] *Selections from the Essays of Michel Eyquem de Montaigne,* ed. and trans. by Donald M. Frame (New York: Appleton-Century, 1948).

Ten surefire ways to save: Set up a bank passbook account. Join a payroll deduction plan at work. Have your employer put your money into a 401K or SEP plan. Buy United States EE Savings Bonds. Buy life insurance with investments attached. Buy investments. Pay off your first house faster. Buy a second house and rent it out. Start a personal car fund. Start a collectibles hobby.

STEVE CROWLEY*

AFFIRMATION

I develop surefire ways to save for a financially secure future.

---

* Steve Crowley, *Money for Life: the "Money Makeover" That Will Help You Build a Financially Secure Future* (New York: Simon & Schuster, 1991).

DAY 130

A little bit added to what you've already got gives you a little bit more.

ATTRIBUTED TO P. G. WODEHOUSE

I*f you watch the pennies, the dollars will take care of themselves* is a true maxim, as far as it goes. But sometimes what's required is the pure courage of a giant leap of faith—for example, quitting a job and going back to school, or into business for yourself. A big decision like buying a house, radically changing your lifestyle, or choosing a new lover is not always the obvious next step—but it may be the right one.

AFFIRMATION

I am willing to take risks.

DAY 131

Make a list of your ten most negative ideas about money, for example, "I have to do what I don't want to do to get money." Select the most negative one and invert it into an affirmation that you want to work with.

PHIL LAUT*

Exercise: Make your list now, choosing your most negative financial idea—for example, "I'll never make enough money"—and then making an affirmation that you want to work with.

AFFIRMATION

I have everything I need. I am financially independent.

---

* Phil Laut, *Money Is My Friend* (New York: Ballantine Books, 1989).

DAY 132

One of the reasons that we adults have so little regard for the value of the dollar today...is that we rarely transact our expenditures with actual dollars....Bankers love it....Because they know that as difficult as it is for us to visualize the real dollars we're spending when we write a check, it's even more difficult when we pay with plastic.

STEVE CROWLEY*

Exercise: Experiment by paying with cash only for a week and observe how you feel.

AFFIRMATION

I conserve my financial resources every time I use cash.

---

*Steve Crowley, *Money for Life* (New York: Simon & Schuster, 1991).

DAY 133

Seventy-two percent of us don't pay off our credit card balance every month....Consumer credit is a big-time industry. The credit card companies and banks have much at stake. Your perma-debt situation is their lifeblood and you can be sure they are quite interested in maintaining that condition.

MARY HUNT*

AFFIRMATION
I pay off my credit card balance every month.

---

* Mary Hunt, *The Best of the Cheapskate Monthly* (New York: St. Martin's Paperbacks, 1993).

I've lost count of the people who have complained to me that they can't find two thousand dollars a year to set up an Individual Retirement Account—one of the greatest tax-savings bargains every offered—but continue to smoke, drink to excess, and take lavish vacations.

STEVE CROWLEY*

AFFIRMATION

I develop mastery over my money and where I spend it.

* Steve Crowley, *Money for Life* (New York: Simon & Schuster, 1991).

To start creating the life you want, you don't need mantras, self-hypnosis, a character-building program, or a new toothpaste. You do need practical techniques for problem-solving, planning, and getting your hands on materials, skills, information, and contacts.

BARBARA SHER*

AFFIRMATION

I balance my inner work with practical steps in financial planning.

* Barbara Sher, *Wishcraft: How To Get What You Really Want* (New York: Ballantine Books, 1979).

Seven ways to help you survive the daily grind: Be prepared with a to-do list. Break gridlock by picking one thing and doing it. Don't try to be perfect. Know when to say no. Control paper flow. Take time out to take care of yourself and do things that make you feel good.

JEAN PARVIN[*]

AFFIRMATION

I beat the daily grind by seeing each moment as a new beginning toward financial freedom.

---

[*]Jean Parvin, "How to Beat the Daily Grind," *Reader's Digest*, December 1993.

DAY 137

The goal setters earned an average of $7,401 each month. The non-action group earned an average of $3,397 each month. Not surprisingly, the action group tended to be more enthusiastic, more satisfied with life and work, and happier in marriage, and their overall health was better....The academic literature on goals...over the past 20 years has shown unequivocally that those who set goals perform better in a variety of tasks.

ZIG ZIEGLAR*

AFFIRMATION

Setting goals can pay me big dividends and so I set them and reset them as needed.

---

* Zig Zieglar, *Over The Top* (Nashville, TN: Thomas Nelson Publishers, 1994).

If your spouse verbally agrees to do something but then doesn't actually do it, point out that the job has not been done and together come to an agreement about when it will be done. If it does not get done by the time agreed on, assume that your mate is not going to do it. Then come up with another plan, such as doing it yourself, hiring someone to do it, or deciding that the project simply will have to go undone.

DORIS WILD HELMERING*

If I had a dollar for every hour of my life I have wasted playing the I'll Do It When I Get Damn Good and Ready game I would be rich. What can I do now? I can stop playing this game and other damaging games and work instead to improve my relationships with other people and with money.

AFFIRMATION

I disengage myself from playing games and use this energy instead to foster financial well-being.

---

* Doris Wild Helmering, *Happily Ever After: A Therapist's Guide to Taking the Fight Out and Putting the Fun Back into Your Marriage* (New York: Warner Books, 1986).

DAY 139

On the most basic level, what women had not considered was just how much their traditional caring values and empathic interpersonal skills seemed to inhibit rather than enhance their efforts to succeed in the workplace.

SUZANNE GORDON*

AFFIRMATION

I create values that enhance my skills in the workplace without diminishing my capacity to care and understand.

---

*Suzanne Gordon, *Prisoners of Men's Dreams: Striking Out for a New Feminine Future* (Boston: Little, Brown, 1991).

DAY 140

There is enormous advertising pressure to borrow money, use credit, and spend more. We live in a virtual sea of it but are rarely aware of it on a conscious level.

JERROLD MUNDIS*

By deciding (when I do not have the money in my hand) that I cannot live without that dress, that car, that piece of jewelry, or that fancy meal, which I charge, I am deciding to borrow money. I borrow money when I do not pay the entire balance on each month's credit card bills. Each bank overdraft costs me money. Each time I use credit to buy a dress or a car rather than save up the money first, I help someone else make money because of my willingness to pay them interest. I do not have to do that.

AFFIRMATION

I begin now to reduce all forms of financial borrowing and to clear up all outstanding debt.

---

*Jerrold Mundis, *How to Get Out of Debt, Stay Out of Debt and Live Prosperously* (New York: Bantam Books, 1988).

DAY 141

Women spend billions of dollars on aids to enhance romance, sexuality, and beauty. Women are used to promote products of sexual stimulation; and women are themselves marketed, objectified, and often victimized.

MARILYN MASON*

Do you try to buy love? Examine how you're spending your cash to make yourself feel romantic and sexual. Do you spend tons on your exterior—clothes and shoes you don't wear—when what needs addressing is your health and self-esteem?

Exercise: Consider your priorities and in what order you hold your health and beauty, love and self-esteem.

AFFIRMATION

My sense of self is not determined by advertisers.

---

* Marilyn Mason, *Making Our Lives Our Own: A Woman's Guide to the Six Challenges of Personal Change* (New York: HarperCollins, 1991).

DAY 142

The $33-billion-a-year diet industry, the $20-billion cosmetic industry, the $300-million cosmetic surgery industry and the $7-billion pornography industry feed…on women.

NAOMI WOLF*

How much money do you spend on clothes? How much time on makeup? How much money on your hair? Each year? Do you feel cosmetic surgery is necessary to your self-esteem?

I have found that the business world is perfectly willing to let me waste my money a hundred ways. I've come to realize that health and a trim body are the best possible beauty aids, that cold cream works about as well as products costing forty times as much, that fifteen pairs of shoes aren't necessary, and that flattering clothes can come from anywhere: Penney's, garage sales, consignment shops, or the most expensive store in town.

AFFIRMATION

I spend my beauty money wisely and appropriately.

---

* Naomi Wolf, *The Beauty Myth: How Images of Beauty Are Used Against Women* (New York: William Morrow, 1991).

DAY 143

Ever since the emergence of mass advertising encouraging people to mindlessly consume—and to keep consuming—Madison Avenue has instilled in women insecurity and anxiety about their looks, their house-keeping, their relationships, even their natural body processes. Ad makers have exploited those negative emotions by offering products that promise to relieve the very feelings of inadequacy they nurtured in the first place.

FRANCES CERRA WHITTELSEY*

AFFIRMATION

I laugh at advertising messages that attempt to get my money by making me feel insecure, inadequate, and anxious.

---

* Frances Cerra Whittelsey, *Why Women Pay More: How to Avoid Marketplace Perils* (Washington, DC: Center for Study of Responsive Law, 1993).

How to maintain the same life-style on a sizably diminished budget: Always shop in supermarkets, never in convenience stores, no matter how convenient they are. You'll save a minimum of 10 percent and as much as 20 percent. No exceptions;…Buy in bulk…[this] can be a great time saver as well.

STEVE CROWLEY*

AFFIRMATION

To continue living well on less I easily modify my shopping habits.

---

* Steve Crowley, *Money for Life* (New York: Simon & Schuster, 1991).

DAY 145

I don't know much about being a millionaire, but I'll bet I'd be darling at it.

DOROTHY PARKER*

AFFIRMATION

I'd be a darling millionaire.

* Quoted in Robert Byrne, *The Fourth and By Far the Most Recent 637 Best Things Anybody Ever Said* (New York: Atheneum, 1990).

DAY 146

Every business day, after a telephone conference call at 11:15 A.M., the Federal Reserve Bank of New York…buys U.S. government securities from major banks and brokerage houses, or sells some—usually U.S. Treasury bills, which in effect are government promissory notes. Say today the Fed buys a hundred million dollars in Treasury bills….

But where did the Fed get that hundred million dollars?

"We created it," a Fed official tells me.

PETER T. WHITE*

Ever wondered where money came from? This is how ours is created. They run the printing presses.

AFFIRMATION

Each day my level of economic understanding increases and my financial independence grows.

* Peter T. White, "The Power of Money," *National Geographic,* January 1993.

DAY 147

I always tried to turn obstacles around so I wouldn't look at them as negative.

ANN LIGUORI*

Devastated at being laid off from her dream job as a radio broadcaster, Ann Liguori decided to turn defeat into victory by launching her own show. She got on the phone with experts, hung in there until she found a sponsor, and now, in her early thirties, she is the only woman to host, produce, sell and distribute her own nationally syndicated sports interview show.

Exercise: Try this experiment. Take a pen or pencil and in the margins of this page list everything good that has happened to you as a result of your negative thinking. If you're like me, it's a very short list!

AFFIRMATION

I turn problems into opportunities for advancement.

---

* Quoted in Barbara Block, "The Right Moves," *Gainesville Sun,* October 6, 1991.

DAY 148

An enabler is someone who makes it easier for you to keep debting—usually a relative or friend, sometimes a business associate. Most often, an enabler is well meaning. He or she cares about you. He or she wants to help you out of a tight spot. So they lend you money. But all that loan really does is get you deeper into debt.

JERROLD MUNDIS*

Self-help books have done us all a big favor by bringing to light the practice of enabling. At one time an enabler was given names like *long-suffering, a good woman,* or *martyr.* Many women are learning that being an enabler costs money, time, and energy that can be better spent. Whether you are an enabler or the one being enabled, you'll do good things for yourself by working toward a loving independence.

AFFIRMATION

Regardless of another's good intentions, my unconscious mind blocks all those who enable me to stay in debt.

---

* Jerrold Mundis, *How to Get Out of Debt, Stay Out of Debt and Live Prosperously* (New York: Bantam Books, 1988).

DAY 149

In the class we spoke of hell as absence of being. I saw that this is how I become when I am shopping. I actually disappear!

WOMAN QUOTED BY JACOB NEEDLEMAN*

This is addiction. Addiction, I would argue, that is fostered by Madison Avenue advertising and foisted particularly on women. The woman quoted goes on to tell that she realizes that she is actually buying a fantasy: this blouse will make me beautiful; that shirt for my husband will make him love me. Fantasy. Erica Jong tells of being in Saks looking at all the women shopping in a frenzy. Suddenly, she saw that these women, including herself at that moment, were shopping as a substitute for sex. Her reaction was to get the hell out of Saks and hunt up a current lover. When you're shopping, think about *why* you're shopping.

AFFIRMATION
I make every effort to discover my addictions and their sources.

---

*Jacob Needleman, *Money and the Meaning of Life* (New York: Doubleday, 1991).

DAY 150

There are groups for compulsive spenders now. Shoppers/Overspenders/Debtors anonymous—take advantage of them. You have the right to feel good about you. What you have is a compulsion of some kind. To love yourself is the basis of all recovery regardless of the problem.

YVONNE KAYE*

Exercise: Write down what you spend. If you are out of control and mired in debt, get help quickly. If you can't find Shoppers/Overspenders/Debtors Anonymous go to Co-dependents Anonymous or other self-help groups—or talk with a friend.

AFFIRMATION

I courageously face and handle all compulsions which compromise my financial independence.

---

* Yvonne Kaye, *Credit, Cash and Co-dependency* (Deerfield Beach, FL: Health Communications, 1991).

A ratchet is a device that preserves gains. It allows a wheel to turn forward but prevents it from slipping backward.

MAX GUNTHER*

"Lucky people have a built-in ratchet device," says Max Gunther. "They keep going when they're winning but when things go sour they bail out quickly."

I'm cultivating this ratchet device in my struggle with self-defeating behavior. In the past when such behavior was triggered, I would not only find myself unable to continue on my forward path but after I would make big messes I would then have to clean up *before* I could return to the task at hand. Since I've learned about the ratchet device, I may not always be able to go forward as steadily as I would like, but I've almost given up making those messes. For example, when I put myself in the wrong financial investment for my temperament (too much risk), I get out quickly.

AFFIRMATIONS

- *I remember the ratchet effect and I do everything I can to preserve my forward financial gains.*
- *When it comes to investments I always move forward.*

---

* Max Gunther, *How to Get Lucky* (New York: Stein & Day, 1986).

DAY 152

One single woman psychologist had $25,000 to invest and went to see a highly recommended financial consultant....He made her feel she was wasting his time, and finally said her $25,000 was too small a sum with which to bother. "Why don't you just go out and spend it?" he asked. She left...determined to learn something about money management and make the $25,000 grow.

CHARLOTTE E. THOMPSON*

AFFIRMATION

I learn how to invest now in preparation for managing my extra money.

* Charlotte E. Thompson, *Single Solutions* (New York: Ivy Books, 1990).

DAY 153

Investing has nothing to do with get-rich-quick schemes or making a killing in the market. It's putting money to work for you, rather than you working for it.

JERROLD MUNDIS*

The leap from *saving* to *investment* is a big one. We may need a safe space in our lives before we can step beyond *gathering* money to *safely putting it to work.*

However, there's no rule that says we have to educate ourselves in a day. Or follow the first advice we get. Just as no one except us is responsible for keeping excess cash in a checking or savings account, so no one except us is responsible for finding investments that pay better dividends.

AFFIRMATION

Cash is a tool. I learn how to put it to work.

---

* Jerrold Mundis, *How to Get Out of Debt, Stay Out of Debt and Live Prosperously* (New York: Bantam Books, 1988).

DAY 154

Remember that, in general, CPAs are not financial advisors. I remember when my trusted but cautious CPA in another town advised me not to buy a house when I moved. The house that I purchased, against his advice, turned out to be the best financial decision I have ever made because of its rapid gain in value....Many women need both a financial planner and a broker.

CHARLOTTE E. THOMPSON[*]

AFFIRMATION

I get the help I need to make the investments I want.

---

[*] Charlotte E. Thompson, *Single Solutions* (New York: Ivy Books, 1990).

Your task is not to devise the most ingenious investment plan ever conceived. Rather your task is to create a plan that suits you and stick with it. For most people who start with a small amount, the best chance to acquire measurable wealth lies in developing the habit of adding something to the pot on a regular basis and putting the money where it can do the most for you.

THEODORE J. MILLER[*]

AFFIRMATION

I save on a regular basis and always put my money where it helps me.

---

[*] Theodore J. Miller, *Invest Your Way to Wealth* (Washington, DC: Kiplinger Books, 1994).

DAY 156

Mutual funds offer the investor an incredible service. None of us has the time to analyze individual companies. And even if we do have the time, our knowledge is not sufficient to make judgments on different industries. Mutual funds do all the hard work for us.

STEPHEN M. POLLAN AND MARK LEVINE*

The idea behind mutual funds is simple: spread the risk. Instead of sinking all your investment cash in one company and rising or falling with its fortune, mutual funds pick stock in many companies. With a mutual fund, if company X goes belly-up, you have companies Y and Z to fall back on. Mutual funds specialize in different areas such as growth or income, and may be "load" (you pay a commission up front to buy shares) or "no load" (you don't pay a commission). Of course, as we are learning, nothing is this simple: some mutual funds say they're no load and hide costs in the fine print; some mutual fund managers are fabulous one year but pick all the losers the next year.

Exercise: This week I investigate mutual funds by browsing through some books and business magazines and calling some mutual fund companies.

AFFIRMATION

I learn about mutual funds with ease and understanding.

---

* Stephen M. Pollan and Mark Levine, *The Business of Living* (New York: Simon & Schuster, 1991).

Don't trust brokers who put you in this stock or that; they make their money "churning" and moving your investment. Look for an investor who has long-term clients, and who picks an investment with the expectation that the money will stay in place earning for five to ten years before it is changed.

NORM LACOE*

A hard time in our financial lives comes when we must decide how to invest excess funds. Some of us solve this problem quite easily by never having any excess. Or we leave money in checking accounts when higher interest is available. Or our extra cash supports people who can and should paddle their own canoes.

We can decide to invest for ourselves and learn how to do it. Classes, networking, library research, and talking with others pays off. A smart broker can improve your financial life, or you can learn the long-term financial benefits of owning real estate. Because these decisions must be tailor-made to your age, personality, prospects, dreams, politics, and geographic area, you must be careful. But not so careful that you do nothing.

AFFIRMATION

I relish my opportunity to invest my resources. I invest wisely, learning from any mistakes.

---

* Norm LaCoe, *LaCoe's Forms for Pleading Under Florida Rules of Civil Procedure* (Norcross, GA: Harrison, 1992).

DAY 158

I don't like dentists who sell used parachutes, and I have a deep visceral contempt for tax preparers, accountants, or CPAs who sell limited partnerships.

MALCOLM BERKO*

Books on finance and money begin to sound the same after a while. *Be careful who you allow to manage your money. Make sure that person is well trained in the area and has her mind on your best long-term interests and not her commission.*

Look for a financial advisor who makes her money from a small commission on your profits; that is, if you don't make money, she doesn't make money. If she can't figure how to make you money, she won't make money.

AFFIRMATION

I find only well-trained financial advisors who have my best interests at heart.

---

* Malcolm Berko, "Limited Partnership Doesn't Pay That Well," *Gainesville Sun,* April 27, 1992.

She became a story seeking a listener.

A "financial planner" was happy to listen to such a woman, to step into the empty decision-making role. He found it amazingly simple to offer solicitous advice, to issue instructions, and, finally, to give orders. She found, eventually, that he became impatient with her when she made simple inquiries about profit. He told her, as her husband did in those safe, happy days, "I'll take care of the money. You needn't worry about it."

CAROLE WOLFE KONEK*

Whatever our circumstances, we must learn to take care of ourselves. Recently, a woman in a money workshop shared a study showing that people who retired with a large circle of intimate friends made our fairly well, even with little money. Those who retired, however, with no friends were perfectly correct in their assessment that they'd need a lot of money to retire!

To care for ourselves, we can educate ourselves; we can find trustworthy advisors (more than one). We can strengthen family ties, and we can build supportive circles of friends.

AFFIRMATION
I learn to take care of myself financially, now and when I am old.

---

* Carole Wolfe Konek, *Daddyboy: A Memoir* (Saint Paul, MN: Graywolf Press, 1992).

DAY 160

As we grow older in an ageist culture, we must make decisions about how we choose to enhance our aging through diets and cosmetics. There is often a fine line between what we do to feel good about ourselves and what we buy into from cultural myth. At this point having a self is essential.

MARILYN MASON*

Ruth Sims gently led us through stretching and acu-pressure exercises. As we moved from rubbing our faces to lightly thumping our thymus (which regulates the immune system), to touching our toes, she was smiling and quietly informative, her manner peaceful and happy.

She was 83. I'd guessed that she was in her sixties. I decided to learn more about how she keeps herself healthy and happy. I remind myself that I do not have to buy into beauty commercials designed to make someone else rich. I can freely search out and follow geniunely healthy and spiritual paths.

AFFIRMATION

As I develop my "authentic self" I become more and more beautiful.

---

* Marilyn Mason, *Making Our Lives Our Own: A Woman's Guide to the Six Challenges of Personal Change* (New York: HarperCollins, 1991).

DAY 161

Make the transition from where the money is currently going to where you would like it to go.

MARGUERITE T. SMITH*

You know what this means: to have money behave as you wish, you have to figure out how you're spending it now.

Give this process some thought and find a way to make it fun. Or make a bargain with yourself: I will keep track of every red cent this month, write it down, keep receipts, sort expenses into categories, and, then, after I add up the categories, I'll give myself a lovely (but not too expensive) treat.

Big categories are: Housing, Utilities, Taxes, Savings, Investments, Food, Debt Payments, Vacations, Entertainment, Hobbies, Transportation, Insurance, Clothing, Personal Care, Gifts, Contributions, Medical Expenses, Child Care, Education, Unreimbursed Business Expenses, Alimony, Child Support. Save one tiny amount of leeway—Mystery Cash—it evaporates by itself.

AFFIRMATION

As the first step in personal finance management, I keep track of my spending.

---

* Marguerite T. Smith, "How To Start Controlling Your Spending," *Money Guide to Personal Finance,* Spring 1989.

In my years of financial advising I have developed a series of ironclad rules that I pass on to my clients. They are: 1) You get what you pay for. 2) There is no such thing as a free lunch. 3) Luxury cars, boats, collectibles, art, jewelry, gems, precious metals, and antiques are for pleasure, not investment purposes. 4) Insurance policies are never investments. 5) Never agree to an investment, regardless of who suggests it, without first getting some literature, studying it, and thinking about it overnight.

STEPHEN M. POLLAN AND MARK LEVINE*

Playing both ends against the middle, or finding some way to eat my cake and have it, is a fun exercise for me. My secret is that while I follow, as best I can, the best investment advice I can find, I also allow for the wild dream. The odds of my winning next week's lottery are tiny, but my dream and I buy one ticket a week anyway.

AFFIRMATION

I play the investment game to win, knowing one way to win is to enjoy the game.

---

* Stephen M. Pollan and Mark Levine, *The Business of Living* (New York: Simon & Schuster, 1991).

DAY 163

When the interest from the investments equals our cost of living, we reach financial independence.

AMY DACYCZYN*

     Another way of putting this is: how much is your cost of living and can you meet it without holding a full-time job? You could own rental property and live in one unit while the other apartments pay your cost of living. Some women explore communal housing or other creative options, such as being paid to manage an apartment complex and receiving free housing as a benefit. Social Security can be a help, as can reaching the age of sixty-five and becoming eligible for Medicare. Some women plan their place of retirement carefully, considering the cost of living in the area, as well as other resources important to them.

AFFIRMATION

I creatively consider many options on my road to financial independence.

---

* Amy Dacyczyn, *Tightwad Gazette,* May 1992.

DAY 164

Except in a few rare and fortunate cases, the powers that be, in this and any land, are a remarkably uniform set of…market manipulators and well-oiled office seekers.

THOMAS FLEMING, EDITOR OF CHRONICLES*

Just for fun, take a close look at the backgrounds of your city or county commissioners. It's fascinating to see how many are connected with real estate. The lesson for us as citizens and voters is to grow alert to currents of power and of money. We can ask, "Who will profit from this zoning action? Or redrawing the city limits? Do I want to support this?"

AFFIRMATION

I grow alert to currents of power, to where the money is and how it talks.

---

* Quoted in Lewis H. Lapham's *Money and Class in America: Notes and Observations on Our Civil Religion* (New York: Weidenfeld & Nicholson, 1988).

DAY 165

Myth: Financial planning is complicated.

Reality: Unless you want to get your hands dirty and do the research yourself, financial planning is no more complicated than finding good, socially responsible professional advice and following it.

JACK A. BRILL AND ALAN REDER*

Have you ever gone swimming in cold spring water on a hot summer day? Stick a toe in and you're likely to yank it out saying, "Oh, this is cold." Dive in all at once or inch yourself in, and a few minutes later you'll probably find you are enjoying yourself. A difficult swim today becomes an easy one tomorrow. Finding your financial way does get easier. And choosing a financial path with heart (socially responsible investing) can give us more reasons than piling up the money to become good stewards of our financial affairs.

AFFIRMATION

I find the professional advice I need in achieving financial independence.

---

* Jack A. Brill and Alan Reder, *Investing from the Heart: The Guide to Socially Responsible Investments and Money Management* (New York: Crown Publishers, 1992).

To obtain retirement benefits for you and your dependents, you have to accumulate 40 credits by working at least 10 years. Once you obtain 40 credits, you are fully insured for the rest of your life, even if you haven't worked for years before you begin to collect benefits.

TOM AND NANCY BIRACREE*

The rules for collecting Social Security are straightforward. We can collect benefits by working ourselves or by being married, or divorced, from a qualified wage earner. The stakes are high; it behooves all women to learn what the rules are, how they apply to us personally, and, most importantly, to take the necessary steps early to see that we are covered.

AFFIRMATION

I educate myself about Social Security and share the information with others.

---

* Tom Biracree and Nancy Biracree, *Over Fifty: The Resource Book for the Better Half of Your Life* (New York: Harper Perennial, 1991).

DAY 167

So let's forget the ugly defeatist word budget. *Yuck! What I want has nothing to do with budgeting; let's call it repositioning. I want you to 1) know what you spend; 2) know how you allocate your income in terms of percentages; 3) prioritize your spending in terms of satisfaction; and 4) reposition your low-priority expenditures toward investments.*

ADRIANE G. BERG*

While Adriane Berg wrote her book for younger women, women start their financial lives at various times and come to financial consciousness at all ages. If you don't have your financial house in tip-top order, why not start at the beginning?

AFFIRMATION
I pay myself first.

---

* Adriane G. Berg, *Your Wealth Building Years: Financial Planning for 18 to 38 Year Olds* (New York: New Market Press, 1986, 1991).

The heels are worn down, the soles are thin, but the shoe tops still look great. Time to throw out the shoes, right? Wrong. If the shoes are good-quality leather, take them in for repair. Repairs cost only a fraction of the price of a new pair.

RODALE PRESS*

Exercise: Consider purging your possessions, having a garage sale, and/or donating (with a receipt for tax deduction) those unwanted things to charity.

AFFIRMATION

I avoid mindless consumerism by getting the most from all my possessions.

---

* *Cut Your Bills in Half* (Emmaus, PA: Rodale Press, 1989).

DAY 169

Do those time-consuming thrifty things.

AMY DACYCZYN*

In the *Tightwad Gazette,* Amy Dacyczyn tells of her husband who spent nine hours to call twenty-two car dealerships. He saved $4,000 off the sticker price. "However," she says, "he would not stop at twenty-two department stores to save a few cents on Scotch tape."

Amy Dacyczyn also suggests that when money-saving activities conflict with quality family time you can solve the dilemma by choosing activities that meet both needs, such as planting and caring for a garden or building something.

She proposes that we "think about the spare minutes as small change that accumulates. Use those moments to accomplish small tasks," she says. A favorite of mine is, "double up on activities"—for example, iron or do hand sewing while watching TV.

AFFIRMATION

I encourage my use of time to save me money and my use of money to save me time.

---

* Amy Dacyczyn, *Tightwad Gazette,* July 1991.

DAY 170

The populace may hiss me, but when I go home and think of my money, I applaud myself.

HORACE*

    Some of us remember what they used to say about Liberace with his lispy manner, flamboyant air, and rhinestone suits—that he cried all the way to the bank. When we have our own priorities clearly in mind, ignoring disparaging remarks is easy.

AFFIRMATION

How others feel about my financial priorities is unimportant.

---

* Quoted in Lewis H. Lapham's *Money and Class in America: Notes and Observations on Our Civil Religion* (New York: Weidenfeld & Nicolson, 1988).

DAY 171

Any serious search for self-knowledge and self-development requires that we study the meaning that money actually has for us.

JACOB NEEDLEMAN*

AFFIRMATION

In my desire for financial awareness I learn the meaning money has for me.

---

* Jacob Needleman, *Money and the Meaning of Life* (New York: Doubleday, 1991).

From my own survey of two hundred separated or divorced people, the average time of recovery was seven years; many respondents wrote that twenty and thirty years after terminating their relationships, they are still reeling from the emotional wallop.

DIANE MEDVED[*]

No matter how friendly, divorce is traumatic. And costly.

AFFIRMATION
I carefully calculate the costs, financial and emotional, of leaving a committed marriage or relationship.

[*] Diane Medved, *The Case Against Divorce* (New York: Donald Fine, 1989).

Even today, it is surprising how many people—usually women—rely on their partners to set everything up fairly. That can be a recipe for financial and emotional disaster.

NEIL HUROWITZ[*]

There we go again mixing romance and money. Expecting someone to take care of us. Thinking life will be fair and that a great father-god sits up there somewhere, benevolently handing out goodies to all the girls who have been good.

Years later, we can wake up after a divorce or separation to find ourselves grown up, alone, and poor. Getting yourself secure financially is one way to ensure it won't happen to you.

Hopefully, you won't find yourself negotiating a settlement. But if you do, Hurowitz says every divorce should "involve two attorneys, two accountants and two of any other professional that might be necessary—one for each side, as in a business discussion."

Exercise: Take time to review the financial costs and rewards of your marital, family, and romantic involvements.

AFFIRMATION
I rely on myself for my financial future.

---

[*] Neil Hurowitz, *How to Get a Fair Shake From an Unfair Spouse* (King of Prussia, PA: Law-Trac Press, 1991).

DAY 174

Financial Freedom is when you never do anything that you don't want to do for money and you never omit doing something that you want to do because of lack of money.

PHIL LAUT[*]

Never doing anything for money that you don't want to do is a pretty broad creed. I am always making judicious trades of my time and energy for money. And money at times buys me time and energy. The trick is to not be forced into trades you don't agree with.

AFFIRMATION

I know what financial freedom is for me, and I obtain it.

---

[*] Phil Laut, *Money Is My Friend* (New York: Ballantine Books, 1989).

DAY 175

Any woman who has ever managed a home and family is fully aware that it is a job without pay which requires, as one of my students wrote, that we provide the skills of "money management, house maintenance, social director, nurse, intermediary, transportation expert, decorator, cultural expert, psychologist, and family-relations and child-development specialist. We deal," she concluded, "with the reality of maintaining life."

LEE MORICAL[*]

Balancing roles does not come easily: self and career; self and marriage or relationship; self and children. For most, these roles are at the very core of our lives. To add monetary considerations seems an imposition; surely our loved ones will take care of us as we took care of them. Yet, if we do not value ourselves—our time, our energy, our commitment—who will?

AFFIRMATION
I own my worth and my value.

---

[*] Lee Morical, *Where's My Happy Ending? Women and the Myth of Having It All* (Reading, MA: Addison-Wesley, 1984).

DAY 176

Despite all its complex rules and variations, the money game is essentially very simple. It is the business of using money to make money.

ANNE KOHN BLAU*

You need money to make money; it's as plain as that. This is the true meaning of those charts and tables that prove if you've saved a dollar a day, and invested it since you were two days old, by the time you're seventy, you'll be a billionaire!

The ordinary individual quickly learns, however, that the nitty-gritty of accumulating money is hard work. When you start from zero, from non-moneyed people, without a mentor or spectacular talent—and the luck and ability to capitalize on them—staying in the no-win position of not accumulating money can be temptingly easy.

AFFIRMATION

I am learning to use money to make money.

---

* Anne Kohn Blau, *The Sex of the Dollar: Street-Smart Financial Planning for Women* (New York: Simon & Schuster, 1988).

DAY 177

With money in your pocket, you are wise and you are handsome and you sing well, too.

YIDDISH PROVERB*

Once you get the hang of it, you'll discover that ways of saving money are all around you. Your bank, for example, is a good place to begin. A good book to read is *The Bank Book: How to Revoke Your Bank's License to Steal*. Or go to your library and read Mrkvicka's "Twelve Ways to Avoid Being Ripped Off by Your Bank" in *Bottom Line Personal*. He suggests banking tactics like: never borrow on a typical installment loan basis; don't allow the bank to force you to make payments into a bank escrow fund for your home insurance and property taxes; use a small bank rather than a big one (small banks tend to be more flexible; you are more important to them).

Exercise: Today learn something new about your bank operations. A priority is to introduce yourself and make some first-name friends at your bank.

AFFIRMATION

Each day I discover more ways to save money.

---

* Edward F. Mrkvicka, Jr., *The Bank Book: How to Revoke Your Bank's License to Steal* (New York: HarperCollins, 1992).

DAY 178

Now I wonder, why did I give away my power by "asking"? I could have told him what I planned to do with the money. By training and role expectation, women frequently hand the power to men without realizing it.

Natalie Rogers[*]

Natalie Rogers talks of the small amounts of money she earned in her marriage from part-time jobs and how without thinking she handed over both money and power. Creating goals of her own would have empowered her, kept her energy in her own hands. With a self-chosen goal she might have decided to work more hours and to reach her goal sooner, or found that she needed more education to reach it.

Some women rush to give away whatever they have. Do you?

AFFIRMATION

I am in control of my own finances.

---

[*] Natalie Rogers, *Emerging Woman: A Decade of Midlife Transitions* (Point Reyes, CA: Personal Press, 1980).

A smart woman also knows that she should never be so blinded…that she fails to pay attention to any of the following: his attitude towards women in general—his attitude towards money.…

STEVEN CARTER AND JULIA SOKOL*

In many ways, today the discussion of money is what the discussion of sex used to be: taboo—never mentioned in polite society.

Marriage is, among other things, a business contract. It's not smart to go into business with a partner you don't know a lot about. Smart women know that the time to talk about budgets, goals, and how a baby would be cared for and paid for is before marriage.

Exercise: Clarify your money situation with your partner.

AFFIRMATION

I approach the business of marriage as I do any other financial contract—mindfully.

---

* Steven Carter and Julia Sokol, *What Smart Women Know* (New York: Dell, 1990).

DAY 180

If no one else gives me value, I give it to myself.

Jo Ann Lordahl[*]

Recently, a long overdue insight came to me. After a series of family dinners, many in my home, some in restaurants (all enjoyable), I finally, truly, saw a connection between my time and energy spent in shopping, cooking, cleaning up, and the fact that my so-called free labor was saving somebody money! The restaurants received cash for their services. I was paid in verbal appreciation and by my pleasure in providing for my family and friends. I also noticed that the dinners cost me time and energy that I could have spent on my paid work.

The number of dinners I host may not change. But my attitude toward them has.

AFFIRMATION

I spend my time and energy in ways that please me.

---

[*] Jo Ann Lordahl, *The End of Motherhood: New Identities, New Lives* (Deerfield Beach, FL: Health Communications, 1990).

Although well known as an artist, the late Andy Warhol perhaps deserved to be better known as a businessman. He arrived in New York in 1949, the son of an impoverished Pennsylvania coal miner....On his death in 1987 Warhol left an estate estimated at $15 million.... Warhol told...how he had happened to come upon the subject of his art: "I asked 10 or 15 people for suggestions...finally one lady friend of mine asked me the right question, 'Well, what do you love most?' That's how I started painting money."

LEWIS LAPHAM*

Read Lapham's funny and informative book and gain an insider's look at the wealthy and the way money operates in the United States.

Exercise: Study how money affects others so you can discern its effect on yourself.

AFFIRMATION

My greatest wealth comes from following my life's passion.

---

* Lewis Lapham, *Money and Class in America: Notes and Observations on Our Civil Religion* (New York: Weidenfeld & Nicolson, 1988).

DAY 182

Ask yourself these questions when you loan to family and friends: Is it a loan or a gift? Who is getting the loan? Will interest be charged? When will the money be returned? What if the lender dies? Experts stress the importance of having an agreement drawn up in writing.

KIM C. FLODIN[*]

Experts suggest that when loaning money, even to family members, we should secure a written agreement about the terms of repayment. And that we make sure, beforehand, that we could live without the return of our money. Andrew Feinberg, *Downsize Your Debt: How to Take Control of Your Personal Finances,* says that 50 percent of loans to family members are never repaid and the repayment rate from friends is only 75 percent.

AFFIRMATION

When loaning money I secure a written agreement about the terms of repayment.

---

[*] Kim C. Flodin, "What Do You Owe Your Family?" *Family Circle,* May 18, 1993.

DAY 183

Learn to be your own best adviser because there's nobody who has more interest in you than you.

"OLIVIA"*

Yes, you will have to plan your financial path yourself. Yes, the faster you get going, the better you will do the job.

AFFIRMATION

No one has more interest in my financial well-being than I do.

---

* Quoted in Judith A. Martindale and Mary J. Moses, *Creating Your Own Future: A Woman's Guide to Retirement Planning* (Naperville, IL: Sourcebooks Trade, 1991).

DAY 184

Managing your life was about doing the small tasks well and doing them when they needed to be done....if you just do the little boring things every day, in some kind of order, you leave yourself with more time.

DON WINSLOW*

Instead of worrying about or putting off washing the dishes or paying the bills, by simply doing these routine tasks, I put them out of my mind. A certain order in life leaves me with time and inclination to tackle more complex financial tasks.

AFFIRMATION

Each day I put aside time to organize my finances.

---

* Don Winslow, *Way Down on the High Lonely* (New York: St. Martin's Press, 1993).

DAY 185

I realized that my clients brought with them two portfolios. One, the financial, contained their stocks and bonds, net-worth and cash-flow statements—all the bottom-line information that can be quantified on paper. The other, what I call the psychological portfolio, is filled with the unconscious beliefs, emotions, feelings, fears, superstitions, and experiences symbolically linked to money.

VICTORIA FELTON-COLLINS*

Money messages from the past can haunt us without our knowing. How our mother and father treated money and how we are like, or unlike, them are important factors in how we deal with financial affairs.

What did our parents teach us about money? What old saws and biases, clichés and wisdom float in our heads? Do some of the exercises in *Couples and Money* to find out about yourself.

Exercise: Define what money really means to you, especially how it affects your personal habits and attitudes.

AFFIRMATIONS

• *I am responsible for my psychological portfolio on money.*

• *I release negative money messages from the past.*

---

*Victoria Felton-Collins, *Couples and Money: Why Money Interferes With Love and What to Do About It* (New York: Bantam Books, 1990).

DAY 186

Long-range goals will never materialize if you always give in to immediate gratification. A balance you can live with and feel happy about is essential.

JUDITH MARTINDALE AND MARY MOSES*

AFFIRMATION

I find a happy balance between my long-term financial goals and my immediate wants.

---

* Judith Martindale and Mary Moses, *Creating Your Own Future: A Woman's Guide to Retirement Planning* (Naperville, IL: Sourcebooks Trade, 1991).

DAY 187

It's foolish to try to save money by doing without professional help when there are important documents to sign, crises such as a threatened mortgage foreclosure, or large amounts of money at stake....When you have a lot to gain or lose, they are nearly always worth more than the fee you'll pay them.

JERROLD MUNDIS[*]

AFFIRMATION

I seek out the best professional help I need and can afford.

---

[*] Jerrold Mundis, *How to Get Out of Debt, Stay Out of Debt and Live Prosperously* (New York: Bantam Books, 1988).

DAY 188

Personal bankruptcy hurts, but if you're desperate, it can save your financial life.

JOAN GERMAN-GRAPES[*]

None of us likes making mistakes and making a big one in public is horrible. But a quiet financial expiration in private can be even more awful. If you're in trouble, don't let your pride keep you from getting the best financial advice, hopefully free, and the best legal help you can. If possible, talk with several friends and experts. Times of adversity come to us all. We can use them to sort out what's really important to us and to develop inner strength.

AFFIRMATION

I can use whatever legal means are available to me to save my financial life.

---

[*] Joan German-Grapes, *Ninety Days to Financial Fitness* (New York: Collier Books, 1993).

DAY 189

I had to face the fact that writing a "morally neutral" book showing divorce to be just another option—a life choice no better or worse than staying married—would be irreparably damaging to the audience I wanted to help.

DIANE MEDVED*

As Diane Medved probed behind the upbeat words of the divorced, she became more and more convinced of the damage that results from divorce. In *The Case Against Divorce* she discusses the following myths that lead couples toward divorce: being single is better than being married; meeting lovers is easy; and play today—you can always settle down later. Diane Medved gives women the real story about the costs of divorce, describing how our standard of living drops dramatically. She quotes Lenore Weitzman's statistics in *The Divorce Revolution* that "Women's standard of living drops a whopping 73 percent after divorce, while men's climbs a striking 42 percent." Diane Medved explores how we get ourselves into considering divorce possibilities and how we can—and why we should—stay out of this situation.

If you've ever thought seriously about divorce, read her book before you scream another word.

AFFIRMATION
I carefully weigh all options before considering divorce.

---

*Diane Medved, *The Case Against Divorce* (New York: Donald Fine, 1989).

I have no control over my money. Until about a year ago, I gave him my entire paycheck. I was given a monthly allowance, which was to cover my medical expenses, my car payment, insurance, clothing, and lunches. He was making a lot more than I and spending it lavishly on himself.

CLIENT OF DORIS WILD HELMERING*

Every time I think there are no more women like this left in the United States I do a workshop and discover some. We can all consider the money rules we follow. We can change those that are no longer useful.

AFFIRMATION

I create my own money rules.

---

* Quoted in Doris Wild Helmering, *Happily Ever After: A Therapist's Guide to Taking the Fight Out and Putting the Fun Back into Your Marriage* (New York: Warner, 1986).

DAY 191

On the river, one person said "You get what you need." Another person said "You get what you deserve." Person three said "You get what you get."

BARRY STEVENS*

    Ponder this quote. Do you believe that you have the money and financial resources you need? Is your current financial condition simply a function of luck?

    Return to the quote. Which view do you believe? How does this belief shape your behavior? Do you like this? What happens when you visualize other viewpoints? Have you recognized and considered any other options?

Exercise: Ponder the relationship between what you think and how you behave and how this affects your relationship to money.

AFFIRMATION

My beliefs support my financial advancement.

---

* Barry Stevens, *Burst Out Laughing* (Berkeley, CA: Celestial Arts, 1985).

[There are] seven money personality types: Hoarders. Spenders. Bingers [who] hoard, then spend in one extravagant spree. Money monks [who] think money is evil. Money avoiders [who] can't stand to think about it. Money worriers [who] obsess about it all the time. Money amassers [who] do nothing else.

SANDY SHEEHY*

AFFIRMATION

I have a healthy and balanced money personality.

---

* Sandy Sheehy, "Money Madness," *Self,* January, 1994.

Love and hatred, eating and sleeping, safety and danger, work and rest, marriage, children, fear, loneliness, friendship, knowledge and art, health, sickness and death: the money factor is a determining element in all of these—sometimes plainly visible, sometimes blended into the whole fabric like a weaver's dye.

JACOB NEEDLEMAN[*]

Money allows you to multiply your powers and to escape drudgery: contrast the number of women you know who have gained spiritual enlightenment from washing dishes with the number who are oppressed by housework.

Money buys you time. Think of what you could do were someone else responsible for all your housework, errands, and child care.

Money buys you beauty. Think of the gardens you could design, the furniture, the jewelry, the aesthetic way you could plan your space.

Money buys you space for compassion. Think of the people and causes you could help and the changes you could make in the world.

AFFIRMATION

I lovingly ask myself why I really want money.

---

[*] Jacob Needleman, *Money and the Meaning of Life* (New York: Doubleday, 1991).

Solo travelers may be burdened with paying the same price as two for a room (the infamous "single supplement"). Since lodging is the primary source of the price differential, research the cost of rooms at your proposed destination.

THALIA ZEPATOS*

Vacations and travel can eat up substantial amounts of money—with no guarantee you will have a wonderful time. If you've always had a yen for going off on your own, maybe it is time to try something different. As Thalia Zepatos puts it, "If you've been waiting to find the right person to go along on your trip, look in the mirror and then get out your passport."

Exercise: Study how you spend entertainment, vacation, and travel money.

AFFIRMATION

When on vacation I get full value for my dollar.

---

* Thalia Zepatos, *A Journey of One's Own: Uncommon Advice for the Independent Woman Traveler* (Portland, OR: The Eighth Mountain Press, 1992).

DAY 195

A willingness to negotiate prices and to accept payment in products and services from your clients will not only expand your business, but will give you increased opportunities to practice your negotiating skills.

PHIL LAUT*

Exercise: Today ascertain what goods and services you can provide in lieu of cash.

AFFIRMATION
I enjoy practicing the art of negotiation.

---

* Phil Laut, *Money Is My Friend* (New York: Ballantine Books, 1989).

"Everybody cries and nobody buys" seems to embody the story of my life. For years, women came to see my art and if by chance, encountered me, told me that, *"my work had changed their life."* Having said that, they drove off, probably to an expensive lunch or shopping spree. They somehow felt that they had *"given"* me something with their words.

JUDY CHICAGO, FRIEND

"I gifted myself with this last April," Carol Greywing says, showing off her fire-in-her-belly woman statue. *I gifted myself* reverberates in my heart as I remember women artists and woman-crafted objects which I have longed for and, until recently, lacked the courage to buy.

AFFIRMATION
I financially support other women's products and services.

The Con: Credit/phone card: Person asks for your credit or phone-card number to send you a product, check unauthorized charges, verify insurance, etc.

The Consequence: Product never arrives or is of inferior quality; or unauthorized purchases or calls are charged to your card number.

The Parry: Never give credit or phone-card numbers to anyone.

MODERN MATURITY*

Be very careful with your credit and phone card numbers and very suspicious of those who ask for them, especially if they're calling you.

AFFIRMATION

I stay alert to rip-offs and cons that can diminish my finances.

---

* No author listed, "The Ripoff Repertoire: The Twenty Most Insidious Cons Operating," *Modern Maturity*, April/May 1991.

DAY 198

Most business problems can be solved if you can teach yourself to look beyond the dollar sign. Business revolves around human beings. We're not all in it for the buck.

HARVEY MACKAY*

When I was first in business, I thought working hard and doing my job well as my most direct road to success in this job or any later job or career. However, experience soon showed me that getting along with people was at least half my task. My sense of the importance of people skills only increased with time. "Five percent of the people cause you 95 percent of the problems," was an axiom I came to live by as a personnel director. Identifying and not hiring that 5 percent became one of my private measures of success (as did not being among that number myself!). Years later, improving my people skills retains a high priority in my life.

AFFIRMATION
I continually develop my people skills.

---

* Harvey Mackay, *Swim With The Sharks: Without Being Eaten Alive* (New York: Ivy Books, 1988).

DAY 199

Consider three strategies to take money that would otherwise go to Uncle Sam and add it to your savings: Buy tax-exempt municipal bonds.... Use tax-favored savings vehicles like 401(k) plans, Individual Retirement Accounts (IRAs) and Keogh plans....Hunt for further tax deductions.

JONATHAN D. POND*

I hate taxes. Income tax and property taxes are particularly distressing. Tax rules change so often and are so complicated. It's unfair. I'd love to put the tax mess out of my mind.

However, I notice that my ignorance about taxes costs me money. My new tactics are to learn about taxes so I can pay less, and to seek the advice of experts who are familiar with my situation—while remembering to keep my eye on those experts. After all, my money is involved.

AFFIRMATION
I learn about taxes so I can pay less.

---

* Jonathan D. Pond, "How to Live Within Your Means," *Bottom Line Personal*, January 15, 1994.

DAY 200

When your property is hit by a major disaster, document the damage immediately, *we hear from tax expert Anna Maria Goldieri.* Reason: *Because of the growing number of overstated and fraudulent claims filed each year, the IRS is becoming more skeptical.* Strategy: *Save a copy of the next day's local newspaper, along with pictures or videos of your damaged property.*

BOTTOM LINE PERSONAL*

AFFIRMATION

By planning ahead, I remain functional in the aftermath of disaster.

---

* *Bottom Line Personal,* April 1, 1994.

DAY 201

One way to control higher than normal levels of stress is to establish goals that specifically determine your direction. By focusing attention on the goal, you can maximize the use of your energy and minimize immediate tension.

GUNHELD O. HAGESTAD[*]

AFFIRMATION

I use the energy of my stress to focus attention on my financial goals.

[*] Gunheld O. Hagestad, "The Family: Women and Grandparents as Kin-Keepers." In Judith Martindale and Mary Moses, *Creating Your Own Future: A Woman's Guide to Retirement Planning* (Naperville, IL: Sourcebooks Trade, 1991).

You might consider leasing your principal residence until you are 55; then sell it and receive as much as $125,000 in tax-free capital appreciation. While you lease, repairs and upkeep are tax-deductible.

GAETON RIOPEL*

Exercise: Explore the "principal residence" and over fifty-five law and how you can profit from this tax law.

AFFIRMATION

I easily further my knowledge about tax laws and how they can serve me.

---

* Quoted in M. M. Kirsch, *How to Get Off the Fast Track and Live a Life Money Can't Buy* (New York: HarperPaperbacks, 1991).

DAY 203

Countless women each year retire with the expectation that they will receive a pension from their long-time employer, only to discover upon retirement that their pension has been integrated out of existence—disintegrated. Unless you know about integration, you may be planning your retirement with inaccurate expectations of how much money you can count on.

PHYLLIS BORZI*

Integrated pension plans, instead of paying both your pension and Social Security, merge the two—paying you less.

Exercise: Today learn about integrated pension plans and if applicable, ask your employer whether your pension plan is integrated and examine your pension plan booklet for any mention of Social Security.

AFFIRMATION

With planning and education I create retirement options.

---

* Phyllis Borzi, "Pension Integration May Mean Income Disintegration For Women," *Owl Observer: Special Edition: Women and Pensions,* November 1985.

SSI benefits are a mainstay for many elderly women. Of the total number of recipients of SSI over 65, approximately 2 million, or 70 percent, are women, and 97 percent of those have no other income....Only about 30 percent of the persons who are eligible actually receive this benefit.

JUDITH MARTINDALE AND MARY MOSES[*]

Supplemental Security Income (SSI) benefits, were established by the federal government to pay monthly income to people who are aged, blind, or disabled and who have little income and few assets.

A major reason (besides ignorance) many women do not claim these benefits is because they are ashamed of needing them, ashamed of being poor. This attitude creates additional hardship for many women. Why should we be ashamed for having absorbed the lessons of dependency taught to us by our society? Answer for yourself: if you had known from the cradle that you would be responsible for your financial future, and you possessed true equal opportunity and self-determination, would you have made different decisions and taken other actions?

In some measure, all women are casualties of our society.

Exercise: Consider adopting an older woman and helping her with information or support. Become a member of an advocacy group.

AFFIRMATION

Only I can be responsible for the financial future of my elderly years.

---

[*]Judith Martindale and Mary Moses, *Creating Your Own Future: A Woman's Guide to Retirement Planning* (Naperville, IL: Sourcebooks Trade, 1991).

DAY 205

Do you want to qualify for a low-rate credit card? If you've just changed your job or address, wait twelve months before applying. And check your credit reports to be sure all your accounts are reported accurately. Look for credit reporting agencies, such as TRW, Trans Union, and CBI/ Equifax in the Yellow Pages.

LUCY H. HEDRICK*

AFFIRMATION

I love to find the cheapest way to spend my money.

---

*Lucy H. Hedrick, *365 Ways to Save Money* (New York: Hearst Books, 1994).

DAY 206

If you're married, you must be a team. Even so, every woman should have her own bank account and her own credit cards, in her name. She must build a credit rating. She also must get the minimum number of quarters for Social Security, for the Medicare coverage.

OLIVIA*

Bank account, credit cards, credit rating, and eligibility for Social Security so you can get Medicare—these are basic financial needs and must be in your own name. If these staples don't reside in the kitchen of your financial house, you should learn what they are and obtain them for yourself. And while you're at it, think of getting yourself a will, some decent savings, and a retirement plan.

Exercise: Take inventory of your financial kitchen and obtain or replenish all staples.

AFFIRMATION
I acquire financial assets that are just my own.

---

* Quoted in Judith Martindale and Mary Moses, *Creating Your Own Future: A Woman's Guide to Retirement Planning* (Naperville, IL: Sourcebooks Trade, 1991).

DAY 207

If your husband disposes of his assets before his death, there may be nothing in the estate for you....You are not being suspicious or untrusting if you insist on knowing what your husband does with the property and assets that have been built up during your marriage. Nor are you being selfish to insist on having the ownership and control of this property during your lifetime.

LOIS G. FORER*

Exercise: Find out about the current standings of all property and assets your husband manages.

AFFIRMATION

I am co-owner of all I work to acquire.

---

* Lois G. Forer, *What Every Woman Needs to Know Before (and After) She Gets Involved With Men and Money* (New York: Rawson Associates, 1993).

DAY 208

"The first thing I would change about my reaction to Martin's illness is that I would be a lot less heroic and a lot more realistic."

LYNN CAINE[*]

Playacting is seductive. We look from the outside in and we comment mentally as we judge the real events. We are the actresses in our lives' dramas and like actresses we play for applause: "Isn't she wonderful—so caring, so brave."

"And so dumb," widow Lynn Caine adds, who admits that she largely frittered away the fourteen months before her ill husband died. She was brave, but she failed to take steps that would have helped her later.

According to Caine, 75 percent of all American wives will be widows someday. That's a lot of women. The time to prepare to be a widow is while you are married.

AFFIRMATIONS

- *I take action now to protect myself and my family.*
- *I prepare now for the predictable life crisis that I may someday encounter.*

---

[*] Lynn Caine, *Being A Widow* (New York: William Morrow, 1988).

Our lives are a hell not because money is so important to us, but because it is not important enough.

JACOB NEEDLEMAN*

We cripple ourselves when we don't give money its due and admit its importance in our lives.

We live in a material world; the more we can realize this, the more control we can exert over its materiality. Saying that money isn't important means we give away power—and usually to someone who won't use it as wisely and humanely as we would.

Exercise: Today take limits off your ideas of wealth.

AFFIRMATION

Each day my understanding about the importance of money and how I will use its power increases.

---

*Jacob Needleman, *Money and the Meaning of Life* (New York: Doubleday, 1991).

DAY 210

...Ours has been the generation of change. Raised to devote our lives to others, we are the ones who have had to regroup and redesign our life-styles as society's emphasis has changed.

ANNE DeSOLA CARDOZA AND MAVIS B. SUTTON*

Imagine that every girl-child was told, from the time she could understand, that she would grow up to have a well-paying job, to own a nice house, and perhaps, if she chose, have a couple of children.

Imagine further that the girl-child was tipped off that at any stage of her life she might suddenly find herself alone, with only herself to depend on financially and emotionally. And that if she had children, she might easily find herself supporting and raising them alone.

AFFIRMATION

I continue to focus on my financial well-being.

---

* Anne DeSola Cardoza and Mavis B. Sutton, *Winning Tactics for Women Over Forty* (Bedford, MA: Mills and Sanderson, 1988).

DAY 211

Often I have been steered to somewhere I wanted to be by having some-one say no. This has happened so often that when I hear no I look around hopefully.

BARRY STEVENS[*]

A problem with low self-esteem is that a "no" can seem to be the final pronouncement. Or we can break our hearts trying to get something that just isn't right. (If I'd been hired for that job I shed many tears over, I wouldn't be a writer today.) Sometimes we have to work so hard just to get ourselves to attempt something in the world that "no" brings relief. "Ah," we say, "I tried and it didn't work. Now I can relax and go back to my familiar behavior."

But our old, self-doubting behavior is what got us in trouble. Let's educate ourselves, instead, to Barry Stevens's view. *No* is sim-ply a place we shouldn't be, or that we won't like. *No* tells us there's something better for us—a higher paying job, going into business for ourselves, finding a hobby we love, constructing a life we love.

AFFIRMATION

When one door closes, somewhere another door opens.

[*] Barry Stevens, *Burst Out Laughing* (Berkeley, CA: Celestial Arts, 1985).

DAY 212

Superwoman: Tries to be all things to all people except herself.

CHERIS KRAMARAE AND PAULA A. TREICHLER*

How easy to glide down the tempting and all-approved path of doing something for somebody else. How lonely and strange to harness our energy to nurture, care for, pay for, and do for ourselves. A definitive work in this area is Robin Norwood's *Women Who Love Too Much*. She helps us understand that, try as we might, we can't take responsibility for both sides of a relationship—whether work, love, or financial—without the cost being more than we should pay. We need to cease to be anyone's superwoman and to put that energy to work in taking care of ourselves.

AFFIRMATION

Taking better financial care of myself is among my highest priorities.

---

* Cheris Kramarae and Paula A. Treichler, *A Feminist Dictionary* (San Francisco, CA: Thorsons, 1992).

DAY 213

The cold facts seemed to be that unless she wanted to live alone for the rest of her life, in a general and rather quiescent way, she would have to hack her way into the best relationship she could get....Miracles did happen, but there was no counting on them.

LARRY MCMURTRY*

These cold 3:00 A.M. conversations with ourselves are something we don't know about when we're young. Nothing in our age-denying culture prepares us for them either. Suddenly there we are—taking a hard, clear look at our reality. The road we're on is either a dead end or we're headed straight for a future we can't stand. What do we do?

This is when we reach inside ourselves and find the strength to go forward—or to change. "Here," as I tell myself when I sit down at my scheduled time to write, and find, unexpectedly, that my writing heart is dead—"here, my dear woman, is where they separate the girls from the women. You do it or you don't do it."

AFFIRMATION

I acknowledge my resistance to hard work, especially when it comes to finances, and proceed anyway.

---

*Larry McMurtry, *Terms of Endearment* (New York: Simon & Schuster, 1975).

DAY 214

Workaholics have monotone minds, workaholic organizations have myopic minds. They go for the fix of the short-term solution rather than risk the long-term plan.

DIANE FASSEL[*]

To govern your job destiny is to bestow a hard, examining look at where you are. To bring your long-term hopes into reality look at the work styles of yourself and your company. Do you work only for the short term? Are your long-term goals defined?

Exercise: Define your short-term and long-term goals.

AFFIRMATION

By defining my long-term goals I further my financial success.

---

[*] Diane Fassel, *Working Ourselves to Death: The High Cost of Workaholism and the Rewards of Recovery* (San Francisco: Harper, 1990).

I'll be a millionaire and then I'll be 3% happier than poor people.

ELLEN DUPUIS, FRIEND

If we didn't equate money with happiness we could get busy and find the true sources of our joy. Spend time actively thinking about what gives you pleasure. When I discovered that most of the things I like don't cost money, a feeling of freedom swept over me. Libraries and favorite books are always there, as are good friends and a support system, if I make the effort to create and maintain them. Nature's bounty is for everyone, as are the small, everyday pleasures of a hot bath, tea, and the daily paper.

AFFIRMATION

I know what makes me happy, and the place money holds in that happiness.

DAY 216

Experience has further taught me this, that we ruin ourselves by impatience. Troubles have their life and their limits, their illnesses and their health.

MONTAIGNE*

Impatience is sneaky, usually striking hardest when we're closest to our goals.

Learning patience takes time. Patience is not long suffering, or martyrdom, or boredom. Patience is keeping your eye steadfastly upon your main goals, not letting yourself be distracted by your own internal moods or the vagaries of others. Patience is staying on a savings plan when you're sick of it.

AFFIRMATION

I recognize when patience is necessary and I cultivate it.

---

* *Selections from the Essays of Michel Eyquem de Montaigne,* ed. and trans. by Donald M. Frame (New York: Appleton-Century, 1948).

Ask an American what money means, and nine times in ten he will say that it is synonymous with freedom, that it opens the doors of feeling and experience, that citizens with enough money can play at being gods and do anything they wish—drive fast cars, charter four-masted sailing vessels, join a peasant rebellion, produce movies, endow museums, campaign for political office, hire an Indian sage, toy with the conglomeration of companies and drink the wine of orgy.

LEWIS H. LAPHAM*

Over thirty years, Lewis Lapham has asked many people how much, in cold cash, it would take for them to be happy. From investment bankers to poets, he has found their answers quite consistent: each person, no matter how much they're currently making, believes that if only they had *twice* as much money at their disposal they would be hugely satisfied and very happy.

When will we learn that *more, more, more* is not going to get us anything but continued striving for *still more?*

AFFIRMATION

I find out what really makes me happy, and I make plans to get it.

---

* Lewis H. Lapham, *Money and Class in America: Notes and Observations on our Civil Religion* (New York: Weidenfeld & Nicolson, 1988).

DAY 218

*Whenever we develop and use our inner resources to rejuvenate, revital-
ize and develop our life and strength—in other words, when we creatively adapt to circumstances—we stir some heroic quality in ourselves, however full of shortcomings we may be in other respects....The
healthiest, happiest people keep growing and learning all their lives.*

MARSHA SINETAR*

A few years ago I devised a long-term strategy to keep
senility at bay: every year I would do at least one outrageous thing.
That year I learned to ski. One year I self-published two books of
poetry and made money on them. With this strategy, I not only
gave myself permission to do something out of the ordinary, I even
had to do it!

Thinking about the role of money and finance in your life, devise a safe way to be extraordinary.

Exercise: Today, create one outrageous act.

AFFIRMATION

I use my inner resources to creatively adapt to all circumstances.

---

*Marsha Sinetar, *Living Happily Every After: Thrive on Change, Triumph Over
Adversity* (New York: Dell Trade, 1990).

Not spending money can become habit-forming.

ANONYMOUS[*]

AFFIRMATIONS

- *I celebrate the joys of not spending money.*
- *I find saving can be as enjoyable as spending.*

---

[*] Quoted in M. M. Kirsch, *How to Get Off the Fast Track and Live a Life Money Can't Buy* (New York: HarperPaperbacks, 1991).

DAY 220

No one distributes her money to others, everyone distributes her time and her life [to] them.

MONTAIGNE*

Women are discovering that time is money, is life. But some of us learn this lesson and some of us—no matter how often we hear it—refuse to learn. We can all ask ourselves—before we do something for someone else—what we need to do for ourselves.

AFFIRMATION

I list what I need and prioritize my time accordingly.

---

* *Selections from the Essays of Michel Eyquem de Montaigne,* trans. and ed. by Donald M. Frame (New York: Appleton-Century, 1948). (Masculine pronouns changed to feminine.)

DAY 221

The only way I could deal with my own guilt in "taking" money from my husband and children for my own education was to sit down and monetarily add up the twenty-two years (8,030 days) I had put into our marriage. Eight thousand dollars would get me a four-year degree. That came out to one dollar a day for each of the days I was a full-time homemaker. That seemed reasonable. Only then could I justify returning to school.

MEREDITH, AGE 44*

AFFIRMATION

Investing in myself is always a good investment.

---

* Quoted in Jane Porcino, *Growing Older, Getting Better: A Handbook for Women in the Second Half of Life* (New York: Continuum, 1983, 1991).

There is a sense of being in anger. A reality and presence. An awareness of worth.

TONI MORRISON*

Some of us are poor. Some of us remember what it's like to be poor. Some of us fear being poor or being alone.

We can write down our fears. We can speak our fears in groups of kindred women finding and giving support. We can band together and use our anger to make change.

AFFIRMATION

I use my anger to help myself and to help others.

---

* Quoted in *The Beacon Book of Quotations by Women,* ed. Rosalie Maggio (Boston: Beacon Press, 1992).

DAY 223

Everyone with employment earnings covered by Social Security should obtain an earnings and benefit estimate statement at least every 3 years.

TOM AND NANCY BIRACREE*

We can obtain a Social Security statement easily by submitting Form SSA-7004, *Request for Earnings and Benefit Estimate Statement.* This form is free and may be obtained by calling (800) 772-1213 or by visiting your local Social Security office. You may also write to the Office of Public Inquiry, Social Security Administration, Department of Health and Human Services, 6401 Security Blvd., Baltimore, MD 21235. Allow four to six weeks for a reply.

Exercise: Today send off or call for your Request for Earnings from Social Security.

AFFIRMATION

I stay informed about all financial matters that affect me.

---

*Tom Biracree and Nancy Biracree, *Over Fifty: The Resource Book for the Better Half of Your Life* (New York: Harper Perennial, 1991).

The answer is to understand that the tightwad life is not only about spending less…it's about spending in a way that reflects your values, and that should not stop if you have a billion dollars. Having more money simply means you can pursue your values in a larger and even more satisfying way.

AMY DACYCZYN*

We're saving, after we make ourselves reasonably secure, so we can spend! But our spending should be in the service of our values, not spending to impress or amaze, or for other false reasons.

AFFIRMATION

I know why I'm saving.

DAY 225

Dr. Eugene McArthy, the director of the Health Benefits Research Unit at Cornell University, has found that negotiating with a surgeon over a big-ticket operation—like coronary bypass surgery—can often result in a 25 to 36 percent fee reduction. How does a consumer bargain with a doctor? Simply by insisting on a second opinion, and threatening to seek a better deal somewhere else.

RODALE PRESS*

AFFIRMATION

Where my money is involved, I always ask what things cost and am willing to negotiate and seek bargains.

* *Cut Your Bills in Half* (Emmaus, PA: Rodale Press, 1989).

What does all this mean? It means beware. It means the medical profession is unsettled and divided over when to perform a hysterectomy. It means the conventional wisdom of today may change tomorrow. It means that "style of practice" rather than objective scientific information may be responsible for your physician's recommendation.

LAWRENCE C. HOROWITZ*

Taking Charge of Your Medical Fate is an insider's chilling and informative look at our health care system. If you live in city A in Maine you are almost three times more likely to have your uterus removed before you're seventy-five than is a woman living in city B, twenty miles away. Lawrence says there's a big difference "between what [treatment] is known to be the best and what is actually utilized in the community physician's office." Since that difference can cost you your life (not to mention huge amounts of your cash), he suggests we learn the initials PDQ (Physician's Data Query). PDQ is a national, computer-based information system developed and operated by The National Cancer Institute.

Exercise: Research costs of major surgery as well as alternative healing methods and always get two (or three) opinions.

AFFIRMATION

I treat health-related costs like any other service I pay for.

---

* Lawrence C. Horowitz, *Taking Charge of Your Medical Fate* (New York: Random House, 1988).

If hysterectomy rates were as low in the U.S. as in Denmark and the United Kingdom, American gynecologists would collectively lose at least $1.05 billion annually. That's an income loss of $32,530 a year for each ob/gyn in the U.S.

DONNA JACKSON*

Just how much will a hysterectomy for a nonlifethreatening condition cost you—physically, emotionally, and financially? Take a few minutes to think about it in money terms: if your money wasn't going for a hysterectomy, what would you spend it on instead?

Before having a possibly unnecessary operation, take five minutes to write or call the HERS (Hysterectomy Educational Resources and Services) Foundation, 422 Bryn Mawr Avenue, Bala Cynwyd, PA 19004; (215) 667-7757.

AFFIRMATION

I take responsibility for safeguarding my health and staying alert to medical trends that can cost me.

---

* Donna Jackson, *How to Make the World a Better Place for Women in Five Minutes a Day* (New York: Hyperion, 1992.

DAY 228

Either you give me estrogen, or the next time I have a hot flash I'm going to rip my clothes off and shout your name!

BARBARA*

Barbara is talking to a conservative male doctor who has told her she isn't "old enough to take estrogen. Or, as she heard it, she hadn't suffered enough."

I remember the astonished look on my doctor's face when I declared (shaking in my ballet slippers), "I'm the boss. You're paid to give me your best opinion. I'm the one who has to choose, and live with my choice." He raised his eyebrows, but he allowed me my right to pick my way through the medical maze.

AFFIRMATION

I do not give my power or money away to doctors who don't respect my needs or my self-knowledge.

---

* Quoted in Gail Sheehy, *The Silent Passage* (New York: Random House, 1992).

Even with good [medical] insurance coverage, it's a rare patient who doesn't end up paying between 10% and 20% of the bill....You can do a lot to keep your own hospital bill down.

CHARLES B. INLANDER*

A stay in the hospital can mean financial hardship for all but the wealthy. We may not have hospitalization insurance (as I didn't for many years because I couldn't afford it; thirty-eight million Americans are not insured, another thirty million are underinsured). Even if we have insurance we may not understand it. *Don't be a victim.* Prepare ahead of time for the possibility that you will need to be hospitalized. Make sure your insurance is insured (listed with your state insurance office) and worth what you're paying for it. Explore the possibilities of getting insurance if you don't have it. Read articles like *Twenty-Four Ways to Cut Hospital Health Care Bills* before you become hospitalized. Inlander suggests we try to stay out of the hospital in the first place, quoting a study that places "the number of avoidable hospitalizations of non-elderly adults at an astounding 40%!"

Exercise: Today, educate yourself about your medical insurance.

AFFIRMATION

I accept the responsibility of learning about my medical insurance and ways to cut hospitalization costs.

---

* Charles B. Inlander, "Twenty-Four Ways to Cut Hospital Health Care Bills," *Bottom Line Personal,* January 15, 1992.

DAY 230

Living with Granny taught me that aging does not make women powerless objects of pity but colorful and entertaining individuals, and on occasion, fire-breathing dragons that wise people don't cross.

FLORENCE KING[*]

Years ago when I was moaning anxiously over how old I was (and how poor), I teased out the realization that only when I was unhappy, not living the life I wanted, did my aging and poverty loom so heavily. Now, when I begin to worry, I've learned to ask, *What am I missing now in my life? In what ways am I killing myself? Allowing myself to be killed?*

Instead of thinking of age negatively, think instead of Abraham Lincoln's comment, "Most people are about as happy as they make up their minds to be." We can all cultivate our character so the quality of our old age isn't solely dependent on money.

AFFIRMATION

I shall age with power and grace and dignity—enjoying all that life has to offer.

[*] Florence King, *Reflections in a Jaundiced Eye* (New York: St. Martin's Press, 1989).

DAY 231

I have four little pensions and so there's enough money to travel, take growth seminars and to contribute to worthy causes. Of course I worked very hard when I was younger.

RUTH SIMS, 83 YEARS OLD AND RETIRED

Exercise: Imagine yourself at eighty-five. Think of your family and friends, activities, and your financial condition.

AFFIRMATION

I begin now to prepare for financial security in my old age.

The risk of poverty for independent women is nothing new; what is new today is the rapid growth in the number of women who fall prey to this poverty.

GILLIE BERAM AND CAROLINE T. CHAUNCEY*

The time to become financially conscious and independent is before circumstances force you to.

AFFIRMATION

I strengthen my financial consciousness now and take steps to avoid poverty.

---

* Gillie Beram and Caroline T. Chauncey, "Money Matters: The Economics of Aging for Women," *Ourselves Growing Older* (New York: Simon & Schuster, 1987).

DAY 233

One-fourth the number of all widows have gone through the insurance benefits left by their husbands within two months; more than half have nothing left after eighteen months.... Yet widows go on to live an average of eighteen and one-half years after their husbands' deaths.

GILLIE BERAM AND CAROLINE T. CHAUNCEY*

Long years as a widow are rarely anticipated by a married woman nor is the notion that the funds she expects to live on may be eaten up by her husband's final illness. After his death she may find herself emotionally devastated and little prepared to handle everything alone.

AFFIRMATION

I prepare now to look after myself when I'm on my own.

---

* Gillie Beram and Caroline T. Chauncey, "Money Matters: The Economics of Aging for Women," *Ourselves Growing Older* (New York: Simon & Schuster, 1987).

There are three essential steps to take if you want to make the most profit when you sell your home through a realtor: (1) Price your house appropriately, (2) Make sure it's in pristine condition inside and out, and (3) Eliminate all clutter.

LUCY H. HEDRICK*

AFFIRMATION

I have a positive attitude when buying or selling my home, and I do my homework.

---

* Lucy H. Hedrick, *365 Ways to Save Money* (New York: Hearst Books, 1994).

Price is no object for supermarket shoppers, says a University of Florida researcher, who found that most people in a recent study could not name the cost of an item seconds after putting it into the grocery cart....Almost nobody could tell you the amount of savings from an item on special....In 85 percent of the purchases, the product the shopper put in the cart was the only one they touched.

NEWSPAPER ARTICLE, *Gainesville Sun**

A dollar saved from *not spending* is fully as good as a dollar earned—better, in fact, because of taxes.

When I was poor, I became a ferocious shopper: hunting bargains without compromising quality; buying foods that gave the most nutrition for the least cost; stalking treasures at flea markets and garage sales. My pet saving tactics still work: eating little to no junk food (healthy, too); ordering water when eating out (also saves calories); and buying whole chickens rather than parts because they're cheaper.

AFFIRMATION

I have fun learning to cut my costs and get the most for my dollar.

---

* *Gainesville Sun*, September 19, 1989.

DAY 236

Market order: You buy or sell at whatever price prevails when your order is executed.

Limit order: You trade only at the limit price you set or better—meaning lower when buying and higher when selling.

JOHN MARKESE[*]

If you play the stock market, you must learn the vocabulary or be willing to trust your financial advisor with your life—probably not a wise idea. There are many books and articles for those new to the market, or you can take a class at your nearest college.

AFFIRMATION
I educate myself about all of my investments or potential investments.

---

[*]John Markese, "How the Right Buy and Sell Orders Boost Your Profits," *Money*, September 1990.

DAY 237

So there I was looking at this silver wedding anniversary and deciding no. I wanted no more part of it. Even with my education, my self-esteem was pretty low. Certainly I wasn't working anywhere remotely close to my potential. I had no money, no job and two dependent children. And I said, "I don't want to be married anymore." Just like that.

This is sound advice: Don't do it like that! Planning is necessary. Save a little. Take some courses. Get a reasonably paying job. Arrange child care. Do it all before you go. You won't get any help once you leave.

YVONNE KAYE[*]

AFFIRMATION
I learn to plan ahead, avoiding costly mistakes.

---

[*] Yvonne Kaye, *Credit, Cash and Co-dependency* (Deerfield Beach, FL: Health Communications, 1991).

If I were to relive my married life, I would still choose to spend most of my time...being a mother. But I would also have a different attitude about my rights to time off and sharing of household responsibilities. I would not feel guilty when I took time for myself to read, write, study, or be with others.

NATALIE ROGERS*

Learning to take care of ourselves is a watershed event. On one side of the mountain live self-sacrificing mothers, wives, secretaries, and nurses who continue, as a matter of course, putting everyone else first. They usually berate themselves for not fulfilling better what they see as their responsibilities.

The happier side of the mountain is populated by those women survivors who have learned to own their money, time, and creative efforts. Cherishing their right to grow, they schedule inviolate time alone for replenishment.

AFFIRMATION

When needed, I take time out for myself and my personal enjoyment.

---

* Natalie Rogers, *Emerging Woman: A Decade of Midlife Transitions* (Point Reyes, CA: Personal Press, 1980).

DAY 239

So many people are trapped in their lifestyle. Money is an enormous part of being trapped. It creates illusions of well-being, or lack of it, so people stay stuck.

YVONNE KAYE*

Once, when my emotional and financial future looked dim, I made a list of things that lifted my mood. I planned to do one every time I was depressed. I lost the list, but the good news is that my depression never arrived. I found that I had incorporated my list into my behavior and was busy doing the things on it anyway. The moral is that you can lovingly plan your way out of just about any situation.

AFFIRMATION

I am never trapped; I always have options.

* Yvonne Kaye, *Credit, Cash and Co-dependency* (Deerfield Beach, FL: Health Communications, 1991).

DAY 240

Never give up…Never, never, give up…Never, never, never give up.

WINSTON CHURCHILL*

This is a commencement speech Churchill gave near the end of his life—the entire speech!

What he failed to mention is that you must pick the right things not to give up on. Instead of trying harder with the same strategy that hasn't worked the last twenty-two times—give it up! Try something different. We may fail forever at saving five dollars a day, yet be successful tomorrow by aiming for fifty cents a day.

Exercise: Examine the routines of your life, identifying what is worn out and no longer useful.

AFFIRMATION

I develop financial strategies that can work for me, and I successfully adopt them.

---

* Quoted in David Cannadine's *Blood, Toil, Tears and Sweat: The Speeches of Winston Churchill* (Boston: Houghton Mifflin, 1989).

DAY 241

Hell is the state in which we are barred from receiving what we truly need because of the value we give to what we merely want.

JACOB NEEDLEMAN*

We are so busy trying to get what we want that we have no energy left to take what we need.

I once knew a woman who shopped and shopped, building up piles of *things* to make herself feel like an okay person—a tactic which, of course, did not work. She also had a hard time giving anything away: she simply could not let go of her *stuff*.

Exercise: Today look at the stuff you own. What do you buy? What can't you let go of?

AFFIRMATION

I know how to use money to meet my real needs—security, pleasure, knowledge, and well-being.

---

* Jacob Needleman, *Money and the Meaning of Life* (New York: Doubleday, 1991).

Remember that networking is a formal process. Like any process, you must go about it systematically. Your first important networking aid is a business card. Simply have your name, address, and phone number printed.

BEATRYCE NIVENS*

What do you do after you find yourself alone and entirely responsible for your future—and you've never been trained in financial independence?

Beginning where you are, you take first steps. You get a business card printed. You think of yourself as a soldier of fortune, an adventuress. You don't put all your dreams into only one basket. You are conscious of your support systems and how helpful they can be. You are a friend because you want friends. You support women financially because you want them to support you.

AFFIRMATIONS

- *I cultivate business and personal relationships with women who can give and receive support.*
- *I learn the value of networking and how to do it.*

---

* Beatryce Nivens, *Careers for Women Without College Degrees* (New York: McGraw-Hill, 1988).

The real issue has nothing to do with whether women wear makeup or don't, gain weight or lose it, have surgery or shun it, dress up or down, making our clothing and faces and bodies into works of art or ignore adornments altogether. The real problem is our lack of choice.

NAOMI WOLF[*]

AFFIRMATION

I exercise my financial and personal choice.

---

[*] Naomi Wolf, *The Beauty Myth: How Images of Beauty Are Used Against Women* (New York: William Morrow, 1991).

It's amazing how little thought and effort most people put into choosing an insurance company....Would you even think of buying a house like that, going out for one day with one agent and looking at a single house....Well picking an insurance company demands at least as strict a standard as buying a house.

WALTER L. UPDEGRAVE[*]

I do not want to lose my money after I've worked so hard to get and save it. So as easily as I can, I learn to protect myself by skimming the advice of the financial experts who cross my path, lingering when I am personally affected, or even just becoming interested!

Exercise: Go to the financial section of your library and find a few books to check out.

AFFIRMATION

Only I can protect my financial assets.

---

[*] Walter L. Updegrave, *How to Keep Your Savings Safe: Protecting the Money You Can't Afford to Lose* (New York: Crown Publishing, 1992).

Judy Rosener remarked that in her interviews with women in the Inter-national Women's Forum enthusiasm was a dominant theme. She said that enthusiasm was how they described the ways they created excite-ment and fun. Women's companies are often fun. We use our excitement to keep the team engaged and eager to participate. It is a way to influ-ence others without resorting to the use of power over someone else.

JOLINE GODFREY[*]

AFFIRMATION

I have fun exploring options of working for myself and/or checking out woman-owned companies.

---

[*] Joline Godfrey, *Our Wildest Dreams: Women Entrepreneurs Making Money, Having Fun, Doing Good* (New York: HarperBusiness, 1992).

The first and most important thing to look for is the company's capital cushion....Whatever you do, do not confuse size with strength.

WALTER L. UPDEGRAVE*

Walter Updegrave shares the above rule for evaluating insurance companies after he tells the story of Ann Johnson, a registered nurse, and her husband, Miles, a mechanical designer. The Johnsons took their life savings of $26,000 and put it into an annuity paying 9.65 percent with a particular insurance company.

Later, at a retirement planning seminar, one of the financial planners mentioned that that company had been taken over by another company because "of losses from junk bond holdings." The alarmed Johnsons wrote to withdraw their investment. *Seven months* after their original request, Ann and Miles got a check—with $2,600 withheld as a penalty for early withdrawal.

Exercise: List every single asset you have, and review each one.

AFFIRMATION

I learn how to evaluate potential investments and then appropriately monitor them.

---

* Walter L. Updegrave, *How to Keep Your Savings Safe: Protecting the Money You Can't Afford to Lose* (New York: Crown Publishing, 1992).

As women we should be knowledgeable about pension plans, for our-selves and our spouses. Careful planning can make a significant differ-ence in the financial comfort of our later years.

JANE PORCINO*

AFFIRMATION

I have a pension plan for my future.

---

* Jane Porcino, *Growing Older, Getting Better: A Handbook for Women in the Second Half of Life* (New York: Continuum, 1983, 1991).

Our divorce, in my opinion, was a product of our inability or unwillingness to work ourselves out of an unequal situation. The person who has a "good deal" in any system is going to be reluctant to change. I chose the only road to psychic survival.

NATALIE ROGERS[*]

The intense changes between men and women in our society have caught many evolving women in serious dilemmas. We are not taught equality nor do our families usually help us obtain it. We have to grow and become independent in difficult situations. For example, a client of mine was struggling to find her own time separate from a demanding family: she had taught them to come to her for everything. When she spoke of leaving, I reminded her that she would just take herself, and her problem of teaching others to respect her, with her. The trick was to stay and solve the problem.

AFFIRMATION

I look behind problems for the lesson I need to learn.

---

[*] Natalie Rogers, *Emerging Woman: A Decade of Midlife Transitions* (Point Reyes, CA: Personal Press, 1980).

DAY 249

Learning not to be afraid has changed my life. For once I feel free to claim what's mine.

GAY-DARLENE BIDART*

Even rich women have problems with money; this article is loaded with information for rich women. *Lear's* magazine enrolled thirty-six women in four seminars led by the Wall Street investment firm of Merrill, Lynch, Pierce, Fenner & Smith. These seminars were about "managing their money in an uncertain and, at times, treacherous economic climate." Gay-Darlene Bidart, for example, could afford to pay the $400,000 asking price of a Manhattan co-op, but instead, she says, "I bargained down. I've stopped feeling guilty about money."

Exercise: Beginning with articles and books, search out women whose financial status informs and inspires you.

AFFIRMATION

I shed the fears that limit my financial achievement.

---

* Quoted in Anne Conover Heller, "How to Make Money by Risking It,"
  Lear's, September 1991.

DAY 250

Then the power of money came crashing in on me. All I had ever earned was $4,000, and we had been living at ten times that rate.

NATALIE ROGERS*

When women tell their money stories there is usually a moment of realization: other people (usually men) have money and can do what they want; I don't have money and so my wishes have no weight. As Natalie Rogers puts it, "So I learned the meaning of the power of those who have versus those who have not: money power. What had graciously been a *what is mine is yours* marriage became *what is ours is his* unless I fought."

By recognizing the power of money we too can decide to learn about it, and we too can acquire our share of money and power.

AFFIRMATION

Increasing my finances increases my power.

---

*Natalie Rogers, *Emerging Woman: A Decade of Midlife Transitions* (Point Reyes, CA: Personal Press, 1980).

When shopping for money, you can go to banks, savings and loan companies, insurance companies, finance companies, family and friends.

MARY ELIZABETH SCHLAYER[*]

I well remember my first loan. I waltzed into my bank and talked the loan officer into giving me a loan for my first vacation. I had a good job and a paid-for car, and I remember mentioning that my mother was a friend of the bank president's wife (anything's fair in money and war). Although I'd never do it now, the vacation was worth it and that positive loan experience has helped me survive several more difficult encounters with bureaucratic loan officers. Securing the best loan for ourselves is a worthwhile knack.

AFFIRMATION

I have excellent loan-getting skills.

---

[*] Mary Elizabeth Schlayer, *How to Be a Financially Secure Woman* (New York: Ballantine, 1978).

What I have come to understand is that it is not in my mind that I'm going to make a difference; the difference is going to come from what I do on the outside. If I produce a successful magazine, for example, people will start to think of me as a woman who is talented and capable. So self-esteem, self-confidence, comes from getting up off your ass and going out and earning it.

FRANCES LEAR*

The secret is that women are doing it—starting their own businesses, that is—a 300 percent increase over the previous five years. Joline Godfrey *(Our Wildest Dreams: Making Money, Having Fun, Doing Good)* thinks woman entrepreneurship is an answer to the corporate glass ceiling. (To learn more about Joline Godfrey, and how she views women business owners and their prospects, read "Rebel With a Cause," in *Working Woman,* March 1993.)

AFFIRMATION

My talents and capabilities find ample and joyous expression.

---

* Frances Lear, *The Ageless Spirit,* eds. Phillip Berman and Connie Goldman (New York: Ballantine Books, 1992).

DAY 253

I don't like money, but it quiets my nerves.

JOE LOUIS*

Many of us take this position; we don't want to grub around with the messy processes of money, but it definitely quiets our nerves to have it.

I've never understood why money is often treated as a "lower class" concern. Why are we supposed to be less than admirable when we occupy ourselves with money and costs?

AFFIRMATION

I enjoy thinking about and discussing money.

---

*Robert Byrne, *The Fourth and by Far the Most Recent 637 Best Things Anybody Every Said* (New York: Atheneum, 1990).

DAY 254

John Kenneth Galbraith characterizes the present economic structure of American society as based not only on the satisfaction of desire, but on the creation of desire.

JACOB NEEDLEMAN*

It is possible to unleash ourselves from Madison Avenue advertising, and it's a lot of fun once you get the hang of it. Try to see how little you can live on, for example. Don't buy things. Look at your own possessions. Go to garage sales. Look at other people's junk. When you're at garage or estate sales, look at what people value, or what they choose not to value. I've found lovely antiques in other people's junk.

Exercise: Today look at your possessions and ask: do I *need* this?

AFFIRMATION

The things I buy give me genuine satisfaction.

---

* Jacob Needleman, *Money and the Meaning of Life* (New York: Doubleday, 1991).

Night Cleaning: Invisible work done by women working for men who have contracts with large offices.

CHERIS KRAMARAE AND PAULA A. TREICHLER[*]

Invisible work is something many women have practiced for years. They get up early. They stay late. They say, "Don't bother, I'll do it later." They don't value their own invisible work or the invisible work of others. They treat others, especially men, like princes who shouldn't have to wait, or go to very much trouble. We don't take time to figure out what we want, or what pleases us.

Night cleaners make some money. But a corollary to invisible work is frequently that its pay is also invisible!

AFFIRMATION

I make concentrated efforts to make visible all my invisible work.

---

[*] Cheris Kramarae and Paula A. Treichler, *A Feminist Dictionary* (San Francisco, CA: Thorsons, 1992).

It is also important to remember the Fourth Commandment: Wear a velvet glove over an iron hand. *Do not meekly submit to a job termination or a refusal of employment....Today no woman has to pretend to be young or try to be beautiful to get a job. Often the threat of a lawsuit is sufficient to make an employer reconsider.*

You can be gainfully employed until you reach retirement age.

LOIS G. FORER[*]

AFFIRMATION

I practice being a wise woman: soft on the outside and steely hard on the inside.

---

[*] Lois G. Forer, *What Every Woman Needs to Know Before (and After) She Gets Involved With Men and Money* (New York: Rawson Associates, 1993).

The Golden Rule: She who has the gold, rules.

CHERIS KRAMARAE AND PAULA A. TREICHLER[*]

    Start observing how the power of money correlates with social position. Notice which of your relatives seem to be the most admired. Do you have a rich aunt, a wealthy uncle? Does their money influence your thoughts and behavior toward them, or what you say about them? Notice how ideas of wealth and fame creep into your social interactions. Can you discern connections between individuals' influence and their degree of wealth and fame? Do you know people who downplay the importance of money while doing everything possible to obtain it for themselves? How about people who refuse to allow "money" to influence their actions and behaviors? Does this behavior help them or hurt them? Does their avoidance of money make them more spiritual or merely more ineffectual?

    Think about the word *rule*. Does *rule* mean to make everyone do what you say? Could *rule* also mean the power to use money wisely?

AFFIRMATION

I understand the power of money and can use it appropriately.

---

[*] Cheris Kramarae and Paula A. Treichler, *A Feminist Dictionary* (San Francisco, CA: Thorsons, 1992).

"She gave her money to men who said they were buying precious gems?"
I ask.

"They presented this investment plan as a special one, limited to a few select clients. It was to pay huge returns on her money."

"And they took advantage of her because they knew she was alone. She told them, I can hear her telling them, 'My husband used to be a financial whiz. He handled everything, but he has Alzheimer's disease. Now I have to take care of everything, of the money...'"

CAROL WOLFE KONEK*

In this sensitive book, Carol Konek explores the problems of our becoming caretakers to our aging parents. Caretaking may have severe and prolonged financial consequences for which we should work to prepare ourselves—before we need to.

AFFIRMATION

As is needed and appropriate, I open my mind and heart to the financial situations of others.

---

* Carol Wolfe Konek, *Daddyboy: A Memoir* (Saint Paul, MN: Graywolf Press, 1992).

DAY 259

In 1925 Paramount reported earnings of $21,000,000; Metro $16,000,000; and First National $11,000,000. Nice, solid, round figures that I liked. I gave some real thought to motion pictures and how they could use my style and personality.

MAE WEST*

Perhaps we should give some real thought to outrageousness! If we keep on making money and doing business the same way then we're likely to stay in the same place. Or go downhill. It once occurred to me that by always being predictable, always being a "good girl," I was not only seeming dull to others, I wasn't even having a very good time myself. What can we do differently? Perhaps we can take where we are and put an outrageous spin on it: Mae West was in a New York jail in 1927 when she considered moving to Hollywood for economic reasons.

Exercise: Examine the role of outrageousness and fun in your life, and how they relate to your attitude and actions toward money.

AFFIRMATION
I am willing to have fun and make money.

---

* Quoted in Annette Lieberman and Vicki Lindner, *Unbalanced Accounts: How Women Can Overcome Their Fear of Money* (New York: Penguin Books, 1987).

There are 2,000 to 5,000 cults in the U.S. today with 3 to 5 million full-fledged members, according to University of California professor emeritus Margaret Singer....It's the accumulation of wealth that brought America's older population into the sights of America's cults. The financial stakes can be enormous for anyone, but most especially for those who have little hope of rebuilding their life's savings once they give all they have to some group.

CATHERINE COLLINS AND DOUGLAS FRANTZ*

AFFIRMATION

I am exceedingly careful about who I give my money to.

---

*Catherine Collins and Douglas Frantz, "Let us Prey," *Modern Maturity*, June 1994.

DAY 261

Increasingly each generation is on its own, liberated and isolated in and by the economy. We appear less like a permanent family unit than like temporarily connected individuals, currently cohabiting.

ELLEN GOODMAN[*]

Do we buy our kids $150 designer sneakers? Do we take out a loan for their college educations? Or do we let them take out their own loans and put our money away for retirement?

Ellen Goodman's eighteen-year-old took his own money and bought his own sneakers. But was it his *own* money? Had he, up until then, been without cost to his parents? Was he currently paying his *own* way by contributing to food and housing costs?

AFFIRMATION

When it comes to my children I know where my financial responsibilities lie.

---

[*] Ellen Goodman, *Gainesville Sun,* November 8, 1991.

You take some pleasure off the top, you pay yourself, and then you pay your bills. Have three separate bank accounts and use them when you need to.

NORM LACOE*

People have to have escapes. Pressure always builds up and something always breaks loose. Drinking, eating, drugging, shopping, working, reading, sleeping, sex: we all have escapes. Some are more dangerous and/or self-destructive than others. Examining my escapes, I once aimed to make them as "inexpensive" to myself as was possible. But I never thought about "saving" my way to freedom!

Exercise: Ponder your escapes. If needed, devise a savings plan to pay for one.

AFFIRMATION
I make all my escapes as fun and inexpensive as possible.

---

* Norm LaCoe, *LaCoe's Forms for Pleading Under Florida Rules of Civil Procedure* (Norcross, GA: Harrison, 1992).

Volunteer vacations are often inexpensive ways to explore other countries.... There are numerous volunteer organizations around the world, and numerous resource books including Volunteer Vacations *by Bill McMillon (Chicago Review Press),* Helping Hands: Volunteer Work in Education *by Gayle Janowitz (University of Chicago Press),* Learning Traveler *by Gail Cohen, (Institute of International Education) and* The Adventure Vacation Catalog *(Simon & Schuster).*

CHERYL BLACKERBY*

Volunteer vacations can be an excellent way to jar yourself out of your routine without spending much money. From Save the Seals to Habitat for Humanity to volunteer work at national parks, there is work to be done for volunteers ranging in age from sixteen to eighty-five.

Exercise: Explore the idea of a working vacation.

AFFIRMATION

I become more and more aware of the fun, money-saving resources available to me.

---

* Cheryl Blackerby, "A Working Vacation," *St. Petersburg Times,*
  January 19, 1992.

DAY 264

Buying even a single share of stock in some companies can get you discounts.

LINDA G. BUKVIC*

This quote says it all: you can buy one share of stock to begin educating yourself about the stock market and also gain discounts on merchandise and services. Linda Bukvic tells us that Tandy stockowners get discounts at Radio Shack, Marriott owners get discounts at their hotels, General Mills stockowners can dine cheaper at Red Lobster, and Disney stock gets you discounts in Disney parks and hotels.

Exercise: Investigate buying stock, and if feasible, do so.

AFFIRMATION

I can spend money to save money.

---

* Linda G. Bukvic, *Tightwad Gazette,* May 1992.

DAY 265

Investing needs change with age sometimes or with altered financial needs, and therefore one woman's portfolio can be poison to another.

ELIZABETH M. FOWLER[*]

With so many people, books, and experts willing to tell us how to save, spend, invest, and make money it's no wonder we want to throw up our hands or bury our noses in the roses. "Is there never an end?" we inquire, finding that even yesterday's solutions no longer work.

If financial material isn't deathly boring it's unbelievably confusing. "Who cares?" can become our ingrained response. "This whole thing is beyond me," we say, "and besides, I'll always have somebody else to take care of money matters."

The fact is, we will have to take care of ourselves financially. A default decision to do nothing will not work. The sooner we accept this, the sooner we can pass through the often boring preliminary stages of learning about financial matters and get to the fun part.

AFFIRMATION

I travel quickly through the boredom and confusion of learning about money and reach the fun.

---

[*] Elizabeth M. Fowler, *Every Woman's Guide to Profitable Investing* (New York: AMACOM, 1986).

DAY 266

Anybody whose car has broken down…knows that membership in the American Automobile Association (AAA) often saves a lot of time, money, and hassle. But few people realize that…for an added fee of only $5 a year, AAA members are also eligible for a $500 payment toward almost any medical bill stemming from injuries suffered in a car, bus, train, [or] boat.

RODALE PRESS*

AFFIRMATION

I am willing to investigate and try unusual ways to save money.

---

* *Cut Your Bills in Half* (Emmaus, PA: Rodale Press, 1989).

Volkswagens didn't disappear after Woodstock but are alive and well and living in California. Beatles, Transporters (Buses), and Karmann-Ghias are still the cheapest wheels around. You can get an all-new (remanufactured) Bug for $6,500. A good used one costs $2,500 to $1,500.

JOHN VIVIAN[*]

Exercise: Cars are big-ticket financial and emotional buys. Do some research to get the best value.

AFFIRMATION
Reliable transportation is a sound investment in my future.

---

[*] John Vivian, "Buying Used Cars and Trucks," *Mother Earth News,* April/ May 1994.

DAY 268

A new federal law may make turning 65 a little more pleasant for people with poor medical profiles. From now on, anyone reaching that age can opt to buy supplemental health insurance, commonly called Medigap, without fear of being denied because of health problems.

MODERN MATURITY*

It is sad to hear a friend tell of staying at a job she hates in an area where she no longer wants to live—because she is afraid to let go of her present medical insurance coverage. She can't afford to pay for it herself.

Simple means to safeguard our health abound for us so we can rely as little as possible upon the present medical system: exercise every day, eat nutritious food with extra green vegetables and fiber, never be over- or underweight, always fasten our seat belts, don't smoke, don't drink too much, keep our stress under control, and get enough sleep. Add to the above list your own special rules for yourself—and perhaps you'll want to look into some alternative health ideas and practitioners.

AFFIRMATION

I invest in my own well-being and am vigilant in safeguarding my health.

---

* Al Cole, "Open Enrollment Law Expands Medigap Market," *Modern Maturity,* February/March 1992.

DAY 269

The Con: Pigeon drop: Person offers to share "found" money with you if you'll put up some of your own money "to show good faith."

The Consequence: You're asked to put your money in envelope. Diversion distracts you, envelope containing your money is switched with one containing paper.

The Parry: Ignore come-on in the first place.

MODERN MATURITY*

It's said that a sucker is born every minute. But it doesn't have to be you.

AFFIRMATION

I never allow my willingness to help others to be used against me.

---

* "The Ripoff Repertoire: The Twenty Most Insidious Cons Operating," *Modern Maturity*, April/May 1991.

DAY 270

Philip Blumstein and Pepper Schwartz, authors of American Couples: Money, Work, Sex, *found that in three out of four of the 12,000 relationships they studied, the partner who earned more had the most influence in any decision-making process.*

ANNETTE LIEBERMAN AND VICKI LINDNER*

To their sorrow, many women have learned that giving up economic equality (defined as a paying job) means they give up equality. Questions of relative worth and of who does what for whom must be discussed openly and agreed upon in any partnership. I learned, too late, that I had made one-sided bargains, that is, had worked on another person's dreams without first specifically spelling out when my turn would come and what it would consist of. I thought I was sacrificing now for my reward later—I will focus on making true your dream of owning a boat, then later you will help me go back to college.

But when "later" arrived, I quickly discovered how alone I was with my expectations. The other person truly didn't know what I was talking about. I had made one-sided agreements.

AFFIRMATION

I clarify the bargains I make. When my contribution continues to be unappreciated, I change it, or I move on.

---

* Annette Lieberman and Vicki Lindner, *Unbalanced Accounts: How Women Can Overcome Their Fear of Money* (New York: Penguin Books, 1987).

DAY 271

The people who save the most on taxes are those who plan ahead and watch for opportunities all year through.

LAURENCE I. FOSTER*

If we're to be rich, independent women, we'll have to tune in and not out whenever the subject of taxes comes up. Even if you choose to pay someone to do your taxes, you still need to know what she's talking about.

The first thing that gets my attention about taxes is that the government is taking my money and spending it on projects I don't support, like the Pentagon and the savings and loan bailout. I know there are legal ways for me to stop paying so much in taxes. I'll prepare now to pay less taxes next year.

Exercise: Study tax-reducing strategies or discuss them with your tax agent.

AFFIRMATION

I easily learn how to pay less in taxes.

---

* Laurence I. Foster, "How To Pay A Lot Less In Taxes," *Bottom Line,* May 15, 1992.

DAY 272

Myth: My husband will take care of me.
   Fact: Most women face retirement alone.

JUDITH MARTINDALE AND MARY MOSES*

In the past, women have not told their stories, and individual tragedies remained individual. Even when we did hear about one woman's tragedy we tended to dismiss it with some mental statement: she must have done something wrong; I will be wiser. Or, my husband loves and appreciates me; he would never treat me that way.

Denial is still a problem. Many of us refuse to learn from freely available information or to see the large handwriting on our walls. It is as if we feel that by looking at an unpleasant reality we will make it so. In fact, the opposite is more true. By facing the possibility of divorce or widowhood, we can prepare for and lighten their impact.

AFFIRMATION

Financial ignorance is no excuse; I learn about money.

---

* Judith Martindale and Mary Moses, *Creating Your Own Future: A Woman's Guide to Retirement Planning* (Naperville, IL: Sourcebooks Trade, 1991).

The good news is that no woman has to remain in a loveless or unhappy marriage. The bad news is that when a woman divorces, her income drops by 74 percent and when a man divorces his income increases by 42 percent.

LOIS G. FORER*

AFFIRMATION

I live the financial and emotional life I want.

---

* Lois G. Forer, *What Every Woman Needs to Know Before (and After) She Gets Involved With Men and Money* (New York: Rawson Associates, 1993).

DAY 274

...increasingly, numbers of unrelated people are doubling and tripling up to rent, buy, or maintain a house.

DOREEN BIERBRIER*

Putting a roof over our head—and dealing with the cost involved with that roof—is a crucial plank in our growing platform of financial independence. We require, we want, and we deserve adequate shelter. We will pay for that shelter. The trick is to make that payment work *for* us.

The federal government gives us a break for owning a house; that is, mortgage payments are tax deductible. And the IRS allows the fifty-five and over person a one-time tax exemption on the sale of a home they've lived in for the past three years. Some states also allow a homestead exemption.

Home ownership confers status, borrowing ability, and is a kind of enforced saving. Buying, owning, and selling a home can also teach discipline and management, marketing and repair skills.

AFFIRMATION

I consider creating alternative living arrangements as a viable way to own property.

---

* Doreen Bierbrier, *Living With Tenants* (Arlington, VA: Housing Connection, 1983).

The borrower is always the servant to the lender.

MARY HUNT[*]

AFFIRMATIONS

- *I do not incur debt lightly.*
- *Through excellent financial principles I can achieve my goals.*

---

[*] Mary Hunt, *The Best of the Cheapskate Monthly* (New York: St. Martin's Paperbacks, 1993).

DAY 276

In 1984 I opened my own shop on my property in a little building that had been there when we bought the land. It had no electricity, no dry wall, hardly anything, but it was old and charming and small. All the money I earned from my business I poured right back into the business. I continued waitressing on the side.... I love my business. I love being on my knees in the dirt in my garden. Everything I wanted to do, I'm doing.

FRANCIE MISHLER*

Today I let dreams surface in my mind and think about how I can bring them to fruition.

AFFIRMATION

I do not allow a lack of money to keep me from living my dreams.

---

* Quoted in M. M. Kirsch, *How to Get Off the Fast Track and Live a Life Money Can't Buy* (New York: HarperPaperbacks, 1991).

This to me is the most invigorating, energizing time in history for women starting and running their own businesses.

CAREY STACY, PRESIDENT OF THE NATIONAL
ASSOCIATION OF WOMEN BUSINESS OWNERS*

Claudia Jessup and Genie Chipps in *The Woman's Guide to Starting a Business* tell us how to do just that. The authors tell of Carolyn Dawson in Charlottesville, Virginia who uses mobile units to bring high-tech medical services to rural hospitals. These mobile units are used to detect heart disease and test cholesterol levels. Dawson is using the bookmobile idea to spread technology.

The book also includes a large section dealing with capital. As the authors say, "No business can exist without money. And getting money is the major stumbling block for all entrepreneurs: money to start, money to keep going, and money to expand." They go on to share many ideas on how to get money.

The number of female business owners is exploding. New ideas and combinations of ideas are all around us.

AFFIRMATION

I am open and receptive to new avenues of income.

---

* Quoted in Claudia Jessup and Genie Chipps, *The Woman's Guide To Starting A Business* (New York: Henry Holt, 1991).

Paul and Sara Edwards, who wrote a series of books on home offices including Working from Home, *recommend that people running home businesses not appear to be doing it as a sideline to family life.*

ALAN GOLDSTEIN[*]

Just because it's not a good idea to have a child answer a business phone doesn't mean there aren't some definite advantages to working at home. You can control your schedule and it's easier to work around children and housework. You don't waste time in traffic and you save by not buying expensive work clothes or lunches.

On the downside, you can get lonely with no one for chitchat or to bounce ideas against. And if you're just beginning, you may be dealing with the problems of starting a business all alone.

Exercise: Explore whether a home business is a desirable option for you.

AFFIRMATION

I am willing to change my working environment, if it is appropriate.

---

[*] *St. Petersburg Times,* Business section, November 24, 1991.

No book about being a landlord would be complete without a chapter on the common hassles landlords encounter.

MARY AND GARY TONDORF-DICK*

Look at it this way: if you are a landlord, someone else is buying, or helping you buy, your property. In a real sense, they are doing some of your work. You have to expect this will cost you time and energy. With this attitude, you can get on with the task of learning what you need to know and doing the necessary work as efficiently as possible. Choosing good renters is a big ingredient in being a successful landlord, as is the careful cultivation of people who do repairs inexpensively and well. And who will work during the weekend for, as a friend comments, "It's always after five on Friday when the main circuit blows."

Being a landlord is a job like any other. Only in this case, you're working for yourself and the profits are yours.

AFFIRMATION

With matters that affect my pocketbook I rarely, if ever, trust only one source of information.

---

* Mary Tondorf-Dick and Gary Tondorf-Dick, *How to Be a Landlord: All About Tenant Selection, Rental Agreements, Money Matters, and Sharing Your Space* (Garden City, NY: Doubleday, 1985).

DAY 280

If a woman invests $5,000 a year at an average annual yield of 10 percent and pays 35 percent in taxes on the interest, assuming a 5 percent annual inflation rate, at the end of 10 years she will have $78,057.61. At the end of 40 years she will have $1,015,732.80.

ANNE CONOVER HELLER*

You think this can't happen? This *Lear's* article tells of a thirty-four-year-old consultant with a one-year-old son, who is saving six percent of her income, "most of it in a tax-deferred, company-sponsored 401(k) retirement plan."

We should wise up. There are many ways to save our money and help ourselves and other women. There are many women now who could start this kind of a "Room of Her Own" fund for their granddaughters, or endow a feminist cause that they believe in. Or support—financially—women candidates of their choice.

AFFIRMATION

I am more and more alert to the power of money and making sound investments.

---

* Anne Conover Heller, "How to Make Money By Risking It," *Lear's*,
  September 1991.

Many people don't think of taking out disability insurance, but it is a fact that between the ages of forty-five and sixty-five you have a three times greater risk of being disabled than of dying. Homemakers as well as employed women need disability coverage.

GILLIE BERAM AND CAROLINE T. CHAUNCEY*

The problem with educating yourself is not that you can't do a good job of it. You can. The real problem is that you won't cover the whole spectrum of knowledge: how can you think of something you don't know about? My book, *End of Motherhood,* is an attempt to consider all aspects of a complete and happy woman's life.

So it is with these insurance and money questions; none of us can think of everything. I once never had, or thought seriously about having, disability insurance. But you can bet that I am now considering it.

Exercise: Look for disability insurance that is guaranteed renewable and pays if you are unable to work in your current occupation.

AFFIRMATION
I don't desire adversity but plan for it anyway.

---

* Gillie Beram and Caroline T. Chauncey, "Money Matters: The Economics of Aging for Women," *Ourselves Growing Older* (New York: Simon & Schuster, 1987).

Myth: Women can't make it in sales.

Reality: There are higher percentages of women in sales than in most professional occupations. In sales, where performance is more measurable than many occupations, the income gap between men and women is the smallest.

PHIL LAUT*

AFFIRMATION

I take satisfaction in learning how to sell myself and my services.

---

* Phil Laut, *Money Is My Friend* (New York: Ballantine Books, 1989).

If you think money won't buy happiness, you obviously don't know where to shop.

ATTRIBUTED TO MAE WEST

Women have been fed a lot of garbage about money. "Concern about money is not nice," they say. "If you think about how much it costs or is worth you're not spiritual," they say. Garbage, I say as I note how the "not nice" and "not spiritual" labels have kept me and a lot of other women from even noticing, much less disturbing, the solidly entrenched financial power bases that run our lives. Frequently, money does make the world go round.

AFFIRMATION

I open my consciousness to financial currents of power and how I can affect them positively.

If your financial fix is so dire that you need a lot of money for a long time, consider "transfusions" (large loans), along with "surgery" (selling off valuable assets).

Sylvia Porter[*]

Horror stories abound about the dire consequences of poor financial decisions. Most money books for women contain examples of women who ill-advisedly spent their principal. The example is usually a widow or divorcée who is either unwilling or unable to change her style of living. Or a woman who insists on supporting, beyond her means, friends or lovers. This woman does not plan ahead to protect herself nor does she realize that others may not be making the same kinds of promises she is making, and may not be there for her when she needs help.

AFFIRMATION

Because I live in a material world, I learn how to protect my material gains.

---

[*] Sylvia Porter, *Sylvia Porter's Your Financial Security: Making Your Money Work at Every Stage of Your Life* (New York: Avon Books, 1987).

It's a good idea for you to make a new definition of "No" that does not disable your sales efforts. My favorite is, "No" means, I decline your offer, I love you, I admire you, I respect you, and I am open to future offers.

PHIL LAUT*

Your income depends on your sales ability, says Phil Laut, who adds that we're all selling ourselves all the time to our employers, family, and friends. Since we don't learn selling skills in school, he suggests we had better teach ourselves, noting that "the same skills are required to sell a $100,000 item and a $15 item."

Will improving your sales skills shorten your time and distance to reaching financial independence? How?

AFFIRMATION

I learn and practice my selling skills.

---

* Phil Laut, *Money Is My Friend* (New York: Ballantine Books, 1989).

DAY 286

It's time to adopt a safe savings strategy when dealing with banks and saving-and-loan associations. The aim: to eliminate as much risk as you can to assure that your money is totally safe—namely, that it is covered by federal deposit insurance and sits in a bank or savings-and-loan association that isn't going to tumble when the first economic ill wind blows.

WALTER UPDEGRAVE*

According to Updegrave, a simple check for a bank's solvency will determine "the amount of capital the bank has, how much it is weighted down by problem loans, and whether or not it is making a profit." In *How to Keep Your Savings Safe,* Updegrave tells us exactly how to do this easy, thirty-minute test on a bank. If the bank passes the test, then its chances of failure are about 1 in 3,000.

Exercise: Look into the health of your financial institutions.

AFFIRMATION

I eliminate as much risk as I can to assure my investment money is safe.

---

* Walter Updegrave, *How to Keep Your Savings Safe: Protecting the Money You Can't Afford to Lose* (New York: Crown Publishing, 1992).

DAY 287

There was never the question, "Will we get the money?" It was, "We will get the money. We just don't know where it's at."

SPIKE LEE[*]

Learning about other peoples' journeys to the top can be highly illuminating, especially if we think others always have it easier than we do. Spike Lee demonstrates a powerful belief in himself and a tremendous willingness to work toward his dreams. That kind of strong belief will help all of us find out "where the money (success, financial independence) is at."

Exercise: Today consider how you can better support yourself in working toward your goals.

AFFIRMATION

Day by day my belief in myself becomes stronger and my goal of financial independence grows nearer.

---

[*] Alex Patterson, *Unauthorized Spike Lee* (New York: Avon Books, 1992).

Rule Number 5: Never be without an up-to-date will.

JUDITH MARTINDALE AND MARY MOSES*

My decision to start a new financial goal plan arrived immediately after my realization that in spite of my financial savvy, I was guilty of a serious error. My will was twenty years old. My new plan includes these questions:

Is my will up-to-date?

Do I understand and am I happy with my health, life, and property insurance?

Am I realistically considering retirement and what I will live on then?

Do my housing and living expenses please me; am I saving and spending as I wish?

Do I earn my money from my chosen work, and if not, how can I change this?

Exercise: Today examine your financial goal plan, making sure it includes an automatic once-a-year review.

AFFIRMATION

My financial goals get me where I want to be.

---

*Judith Martindale and Mary Moses, *Creating Your Own Future: A Woman's Guide to Retirement Planning* (Naperville, IL: Sourcebooks Trade, 1991).

DAY 289

The last thing I can say to you about money is, you can't take it with you. Never let money control you. I'd rather see someone spend every red cent and relish her/his life than scrimp, obsess, and pinch the pennies. There's something repugnant about a person who centers his life around money. It's only paper and it gets devalued at regular intervals. You're worth more than that.

RITA MAE BROWN[*]

Exercise: Explore again your attitudes about money, and the consequences of your attitudes, and devise your own approach to money.

AFFIRMATION

I work toward controlling my money—not letting money control me.

---

[*] Rita Mae Brown, *Starting From Scratch: A Different Kind of Writers' Manual* (New York: Bantam Books, 1988).

Be certain that you are not working more, to buy more conveniences, because you lack time…don't moonlight to buy TV dinners. Often people fail to calculate how much extra they spend because they work more.

AMY DACYCZYN*

It costs money to work: clothes, transportation, lunches out, and those extra treats you buy because you deserve them for working so hard. It's also rewarding to throw yourself into busyness and to be the important one who is keeping the office together.

Your time always costs you money or saves you money. These costs and benefits of working can only be computed by you: you may choose to cut costs, for instance, by taking lunch to work and walking for exercise on your lunch hour. Or you may decide an expensive lunch is worth it.

Exercise: Calculate exactly how much it costs you to work, and figure where, why, and how you are willing to cut these costs.

AFFIRMATION

I balance time and money appropriately.

---

* Amy Dacyczyn, *Tightwad Gazette,* July 1991.

This artist's life, dress, living space and use of materials are marked by the same rule: to shun or discard the nonessential.

CHARLOTTE S. RUBINSTEIN*

More things around, more food to eat, more house to take care of, more things to do—these are not just the rewards of wealth; they are also a road to poverty and confusion.

Simplify. Simplify. Simplify. "Get rid of twenty percent of your possessions," is advice that solves organization problems and can aid your finances. Sell that exercise machine you don't use, donate excess books to charity for a tax credit, or trade clothes with friends for things you want. Look at everything you do and have with an eye toward simplification.

AFFIRMATION

Like an artist I bring order and simplicity to my life.

---

* Charlotte S. Rubinstein, *American Women Artists: From Early Indian Times to the Present* (New York: Avon, 1982).

Whatever her reasons, they made Herman famous. In a decade and in a city when almost everything had a price—and someone almost always had enough money to pay it—she wouldn't sell out.

ASSOCIATED PRESS*

Jean Herman, 69, died in her $200 a month rent-controlled apartment in Manhattan. Miss Herman had turned down a $750,000 offer for this same apartment, forcing a developer to build his skyscraper around her two-room flat. "She was the ultimate holdout," says Seymour Durst, a developer who wrote *Holdout,* a book about such personalities. She took her secret with her; Seymour Durst could only speculate about her reasons.

AFFIRMATION
As I create abundance in my life I am aware that some things have no price tag.

---

* Associated Press, *Gainesville Sun,* April 15, 1992.

DAY 293

The equal standing of happily married couples revealed itself most clearly in their handling of finances. Without exception, every happy couple reported that the money was theirs—*not his or hers. They experienced no power struggles over financial matters.*

CATHERINE JOHNSON[*]

Exercise: Review your attitudes toward money and how these attitudes affect your relationships.

AFFIRMATION

I lovingly share my prosperity with my partner.

---

[*] Catherine Johnson, "Secrets of Lasting Love," *Reader's Digest,* May 1992.

DAY 294

If I can rebuild a house, it follows that I can rebuild my life.

ANGELA MARTINEZ*

Nine women who are all "displaced homemakers" or single heads of households have banded together in Tampa, Florida to provide building and maintenance service to others. They've helped more than 2,000 low-income senior homeowners but they've also helped themselves by building their self-confidence.

Suppose we looked at our financial lives as houses to build and remodel. Suppose we started with only a blueprint and simply assumed we would find a way to build our house of financial independence.

AFFIRMATION

I channel anger and frustration into physically useful activities.

---

* Quoted in "New Roofs, New Lives," *Modern Maturity*, April/May 1991.

What do you do next? The answer is: **you have to go out and gather information**—*that activity which in high school or college we used to call "research for a term paper." Oh no, not that! Yes, that!*

Don't let your stomach turn weak, or your knees turn to jelly. It's not difficult at all. It never is **if you're researching something you love.**

RICHARD NELSON BOLLES*

AFFIRMATION

I easily find the information I need to accomplish my goals.

---

* Richard Nelson Bolles, *The 1991 What Color Is Your Parachute?: A Practical Manual for Job-Hunters and Career Changers,* (Berkeley, CA: Ten Speed Press, 1991).

As for the mechanics of student financial aid, they're the same for adults 25 years or older—who now make up nearly half of all college students—as for younger adults.

JOYCE LAIN KENNEDY*

Sometimes, in order to get where we want to go, we need pure information from a source we trust. How, when, and why to seek job retraining, or go back to college, are important questions. Where will we go to learn what we need to know about financing education? It makes sense to obtain the best advice you can from several sources. Try your library and the student aid office at your local college. Another excellent source is Joyce Lain Kennedy's booklet *The College Financial Aid Emergency Kit* (Sun Features). Persist: keep asking people and checking sources until you find the information you need.

Exercise: Investigate how to pay for college or retraining.

AFFIRMATION

I educate and retrain myself to improve my financial future.

---

* Joyce Lain Kennedy, "Paying The Back-To-College Tab," (Sun Features Inc, 1992). Distributed by Los Angeles Times Syndicate.

CREATING PROSPERITY

In *Creating Prosperity* we move beyond obtaining abundance to considering what we will do with what we have. We stop to hear the messages that our bodies and minds are always giving us. Perhaps what we have is not what we want. Maybe we've moved to a new place or outgrown the one we are in.

Why do we want to manage our money? So we can better manage our lives. What keeps us from managing our money and our lives? Perhaps it is simply our resistance to change—even positive change. Perhaps, though, your illusions about what our selves and our lives "should" be are blocking our vision of what they can be—and our power to change them.

What a great day when we are finally free to look at the way we live unblinkingly and say: "I created this. If I don't like it, I can change it." And then, "I have the most vested interest in changing what I don't like, which probably means I'll have to do more of the work of creating and sustaining change." This may be followed by another realization: "I am always free to choose the spiritual solution. I can look at every problem and ask, 'What is the lesson here that I should learn? (Which may be to howl loudly and battle your way out of a current situation!) Or what must I learn and do to be free from this? Or to obtain what I do want?'"

Happiness and a feeling of joy and abundance can be your reward for getting your financial life in order and for learning what money means to you. You enjoy money. You have enough for yourself. You own money instead of letting money own you. And along the way, you've also learned how to integrate money and relationships in healthy ways. You have taken responsibility for taking care of yourself. You are a financially independent woman, or happily on your way to becoming one. Now is the time you can expand your concepts of prosperity and wealth in the broadest sense.

Listening to our deepest selves and the spiritual becomes our path to the financial freedom of our future. We tune into what wants to be born. We greet our new selves gladly.

DAY 297

There are two things to aim at in life: first to get what you want and after that to enjoy it. Only the wisest of womankind achieve the second.

LOGAN PEARSALL SMITH*

All the money in the world won't help us lead happier lives if we don't know how to use it.

AFFIRMATION
I listen to myself, and I act on that knowledge.

---

* Quoted in John Bartlett, *Bartlett's Familiar Quotations, 15th Edition* (Boston: Little, Brown, 1980). ("Mankind" changed to "womankind.")

A critical part of home-leaving in a woman's spiritual development is the willingness not to know where she is going. The length of time that is spent in that place of unknowing between the old and the new varies with each person....This willingness to trust in the emergent process is, we believe, the great spiritual gift that home-leaving brings to women.

SHERRY RUTH ANDERSON AND PATRICIA HOPKINS*

When the old ways don't work anymore, or we're not happy, something new must be tried. But the first thing many of us do is to grab our same old behaviors and beliefs that didn't work before, and apply them more vigorously. Then we work still harder for we've absorbed all those lessons about persistence. Besides the old way has always worked before.

Or we can cost ourselves great amounts of money and energy by moving around a lot, getting divorced, or drowning in addiction, or by making our lives extremely busy, or we can just cry and be miserable.

Or, finally, we can realize that home-leaving is a stage of personal growth and get on, as best we can, with getting on.

AFFIRMATION

I trust the process of change—something new is always born out of it.

---

* Sherry Ruth Anderson and Patricia Hopkins, *The Feminine Face of God* (Bantam Books, 1991).

DAY 299

Everything is about money when we define money in its broadest sense to include security, peace, war, repression, and freedom. And when we so define money, we cannot but see that our handling of money and its related issues in our personal lives determines to a large degree how money and money-related issues are handled in the outer world.

IVAN HOFFMAN*

AFFIRMATION

Understanding the broad universe of money and finance helps me better manage my personal portion.

---

* Ivan Hoffman, *The Tao of Money: Six Simple Principles for Achieving Financial Harmony* (Rocklin, CA: Prima Publishing, 1994).

DAY 300

The problem of money dogs our steps throughout the whole of our lives, exerting a pressure that, in its way, is as powerful and insistent as any other problem of human existence. And it haunts the spiritual search as well.

JACOB NEEDLEMAN*

If you think money isn't spiritual, I'd suggest you read Jacob Needleman's *Money and the Meaning of Life* quickly, before you waste any more of your time.

According to Needleman, previous spiritual traditions didn't deal with money because money has never before permeated and influenced all human activity as it now does.

Try to think of something that isn't touched in some way, shape, or form by money. We live in new territory and we need to change our thinking.

AFFIRMATION

I do not separate my spirituality from money or any other aspect of my life.

---

*Jacob Needleman, *Money and the Meaning of Life* (New York: Doubleday, 1991).

The perfect [life] plan includes health, wealth, love and perfect self-expression.

FLORENCE SCOVEL SHINN*

For most of my life I've read Florence Shinn's statement as meaning I should be perfect in each area. Perfect health meant keeping my ideal weight, and having adequate energy and no health problems. Perfect wealth meant having enough money and time for a happy life now, while saving for the future. Perfect love included a happy, spiritual, productive, and loving marriage. As for perfect self-expression (before I found my *real* work of writing), my ambition was to be "successful," which was always a moving target.

Lately, however, I realize that each goal in this perfect plan of health, wealth, love and perfect self-expression can take a lifetime to achieve. Travel toward a goal, not just the arrival at it, is the true accomplishment.

AFFIRMATION

I enjoy each day of the journey toward the perfect life plan.

---

* Florence Scovel Shinn, *The Game of Life and How to Play It* (Marina del Rey, CA: DeVorss, 1925).

DAY 302

AA steps were formulated by a white, middle-class male in the 1930s and, not surprisingly, they work to break down an overinflated ego, and put reliance on an all-powerful male God. But most women suffer from the lack of a healthy, aware ego, and need to strengthen their sense of self by affirming their own inner wisdom.

CHARLOTTE DAVIS KASL[*]

Women in all stages of life and from all economic classes are waking up to the fact that our society was designed by men for men.

By also waking up to our economic power, then using this individual and collective financial power, we can advance our woman-causes. To have a woman-supporting society, *we* will have to design it and put it in place ourselves.

AFFIRMATION

Financial success enhances my sense of "female" identification and the desire to create a female-friendly world.

---

[*] Charlotte Davis Kasl, "The 12-Step Controversy," *MS*, November/ December 1990.

DAY 303

Some beliefs may have worked very positively for you for certain periods of your life. Because you have not examined them, however, you may carry them long after they have served their purpose, and now they may work against you.

JANE ROBERTS*

Ask yourself as O. Carl Simonton suggests in *The Healing Journey* 1) Does this belief help me protect my life and health? 2) Does it help me achieve my short and long-term goals? 3) Does it help me resolve or avoid my most undesirable conflicts (within myself and with other people)? 4) Does it help me feel the way I want to feel? and when appropriate 5) Is the belief based on facts?

Exercise: "My life is mine and I form it." Tell yourself this often. Create your own life now using your beliefs as an artist uses color.

AFFIRMATION
I discover those beliefs that no longer serve me and let them go.

---

* Jane Roberts, *The Nature of Personal Reality* (New York: Bantam Books, 1954).

DAY 304

The spirit of the valley never dies. It is called the mysterious female. Gateway of the creative force. It flows continuously. You will never drain it.

TAO TE CHING

AFFIRMATION

I draw from the creative female source over and over again.

A new self is on the way. Our inner lives, as we have known them, are about to change. While this does not mean we should throw away the decent and especially the supportive aspects of our lives in some kind of demented housecleaning, it does mean that…for a time we shall be restless and unsatisfied, for the satisfaction, the fulfillment, is in the process of being born in the inner reality. What it is we are hungering for can never be fulfilled by a mate, a job, money, a new this or that.

CLARISSA PINKOLA ESTÉS*

This may be the time in your life to explore some women-only groups and activities. Or to read women's history of look at some woman-based art.

AFFIRMATION

I allow myself time to rest, dream, and see what drifts to the surface.

---

* Clarissa Pinkola Estés, *Women Who Run With the Wolves* (New York: Ballantine Books, 1992).

DAY 306

I draw and paint from my own myth of personal origin. Each painting I make begins from some deep source where my mother and grandmother, and all my fore-mothers, still live; it is as if the line moving from pen or brush coils back to the original matrix....So my creative life, making out of myself, is itself an image of God the Mother and her unbroken story of emergence in our lives.

MEINRAD GRAIGHEAD*

Unlike Meinrad Graighead, many of us put our mother's songs away a long time ago. We looked, saw a woman with no power or money, and decided to follow our father's path of brief-cases and martinis. Too young to realize what we were doing, we cut ourselves off from our deep feminine roots. How can we know what we want before we know who we are?

AFFIRMATION

I connect with my deep feminine roots.

---

* Meinrad Graighead, *The Mother's Songs: Images of God The Mother* (Mahwah, NJ: Paulist Press, 1986).

Meditation, education, all the dream analysis, all the knowledge of God's green acre is of no value if one keeps it all to oneself or one's chosen few. So come out, come out wherever you are....Forgive as much as you can, forget a little, and create a lot. What you do today influences your matrilineal lines in the future. The daughters of your daughters of your daughters are likely to remember you, and most importantly, follow in your tracks.

CLARISSA PINKOLA ESTÉS*

We women can remain on our same tired path of not supporting women, not fighting for women's rights.

Or we can set our minds collectively on cooperation, on mutual support, and on learning to establish common goals, priorities, and ways to work together to meet these goals. We can aim to empower our daughters so that not one suffers economic or physical injustice. We can empower ourselves. We can do anything we decide to do.

AFFIRMATION

I do not forget my sisters with fewer resources.

---

* Clarissa Pinkola Estés, *Women Who Run With the Wolves* (New York: Ballantine Books, 1992).

DAY 308

In America, success has always meant making money and transforming it into status, or becoming famous. Success was not earned by being a loyal friend or good husband. It was a reward for performance on the job. It is not the same thing as happiness—which is how you feel. Success was brutally objective and impersonal. It recorded a change in rank, the upgrading of a person in relation to others by the unequal distribution of money and power, prestige and fame.

RICHARD M. HUBER*

Do we want to change the system? Or do we, personally, want to work within the system to beat men at their own games? Or, as Sonia Johnson, author and radical feminist, suggests, do we wish to put no more energy into beating or joining an oppressive system and elect instead to place emphasis on supporting and working for our own values?

Suzanne Gordon believes that the "feminism that dominates the news and public debates is a brand of adaptive feminism that teaches us to adopt and adapt to male marketplace values, activities, and beliefs." What do you think? Does feminism help women obtain better lives and stronger financial futures?

AFFIRMATION

I provide my own definition for success, along with the means of achieving it.

---

* Quoted in Suzanne Gordon, *Prisoners of Men's Dreams: Striking Out for a New Feminine Future* (Boston: Little, Brown, 1991).

Women do two-thirds of the world's work. Yet they earn only one-tenth of the world's income and own less than one percent of the world's property.

BARBER CONABLE,
PRESIDENT OF THE WORLD BANK*

Clarifying your true position in the world is not easy. If you are a woman, it is still more difficult: ignorance, prejudice, and discrimination (overt and covert) are fierce enemies. And all the while the individual woman is just trying to make her way in the world, find love, have children, gain some measure of personal security and happiness, and light her candles in the world.

AFFIRMATION

I am grateful for my life and for the freedom I have to change it.

---

* Quoted in Elisabeth Bumiller, *May You Be the Mother of a Hundred Sons: A Journey Among the Women of India* (New York: Random House, 1990).

DAY 310

The plutocrats have organized their women. They keep them busy with suffrage and prohibition and charity.

"MOTHER" MARY JONES*

Individual women have to keep inventing and reinventing female ways of being in the world. Dominant male culture writes our history, leaving us out and making it hard to learn of other women's work and lives.

"Mother" Mary Jones makes me wonder what keeps today's women *busy* so we won't feel our power and act on it.

Exercise: Think about who your heroines were as you grew up.

AFFIRMATION

I seek inspiration from the women throughout time who have invented their own "female" way of being.

---

* Quoted in *Growing Up Female In America: Ten Lives* (Boston: Beacon Press, 1972).

Courage looks you straight in the eye. She is not impressed with power trippers, and she knows first aid. Courage is not afraid to weep, and she is not afraid to pray even when she is not sure who she is praying to. When she walks it is clear she has made the journey from loneliness to solitude. The people who told me she was stern were not lying; they just forgot to mention she was kind.

J. RUTH GENDLER[*]

AFFIRMATION
I call on courage to become my ally on the road to financial empowerment.

[*] J. Ruth Gendler, *The Book of Qualities* (San Francisco: Harper & Row, 1987).

DAY 312

We write [journals] and then we catch up with ourselves....We see this all the time: people not knowing who they really are, ourselves included. We are slow to realize the greatness inside ourselves.

NATALIE GOLDBERG*

You'll never glean the myriad benefits of journal writing until you try it for yourself. The only rules are those you make and you can change them any time.

Your journal is a trusted confidant, a place you tell the truth, where you try out dreams, spill out fantasies, expose your paranoia. This sacred place of plans, goals, and money dreams is powerful.

Try Natalie Goldberg's experiment of writing for fifteen minutes every day for ten days in a row and not rereading your writing until two weeks later. Then find a comfortable chair, have a soft heart, and read your writing, underlining key words and sentences.

Exercise: Begin to keep a journal to discover more about yourself and try out your plans for financial independence.

AFFIRMATION

Journal work helps me develop self-awareness in all areas of my life— including the financial.

---

* Natalie Goldberg, "Wild Mind," *Yoga Journal*, January/February 1991.

Suppose each of your investment dollars—including every dollar in your bank account—could help build the world you want for yourself and your family and earn you a healthy return besides? Well, that's exactly what your money can do.

JACK A. BRILL AND ALAN REDER*

Socially responsible investments let us put our hearts and values where our money and ambitions lie. These investments give us the best of all possible worlds by letting us help others while helping ourselves.

AFFIRMATION

I spend my money, investments and otherwise, in ways that contribute to creating the best of all possible worlds.

---

* Jack A. Brill and Alan Reder, *Investing From The Heart: The Guide to Socially Responsible Investments and Money Management* (New York: Crown Publishers, 1992).

DAY 314

You meet three kinds of people in life: First, those you can help; second, those who are on your same level, mentally, emotionally, economically; third, those who can help you.

When relaxing, be sure to do so with one of the last two categories. Do not allow yourself to be drained mentally or emotionally by trying to relax with those who need your help.

CATHERINE PONDER*

Where was Catherine Ponder when I needed her? Where, in fact, was someone to make me understand that I needed and deserved leisurely relaxed time of my own? In trying to be there for everyone I am there for no one, including myself. In these days of down-sizing and hard work, time to relax, unwind, and refresh ourselves is vital. All goals, including financial ones, will go better with periodic time-outs.

AFFIRMATION

I am careful with my leisure and work time, always recognizing which is which.

---

* Catherine Ponder, *Open Your Mind to Receive* (Marina del Rey, CA: DeVorss, 1983).

DAY 315

One day, miser Hetty Green (who when she died, left her two children an estate valued at over 100 million dollars) boarded a street car in New York and gave the motorman a fifty-cent piece. He realized it was counterfeit and returned it. Green, who had no other money in her purse, was vouched for by another rider. Later, she went to the office of the trolley car company, plunked down a nickel, kept her finger on it till she received a receipt…and about this same time loaned the City of New York $4,500,000.

RICHARD McKETCHUM*

AFFIRMATION

I hand over to the universe everything that I should let go of.

---

* Quoted in Cathy Handley, *Encyclopedia of Women's Wit, Anecdotes and Stories* (Englewood Cliffs, NJ: Prentice-Hall, 1982).

DAY 316

If you do what is best for you, it will also be best for everyone else. The course of action that makes you feel right inside is your highest good. Take it. Your only obligation is to the Spirit of Truth within you. This is the yardstick to follow when your loyalties have become confused.

CATHERINE PONDER*

A friend tells me she got the courage to leave a bad marriage she was staying in for "the sake of the children" on the day she recognized that she was transferring her ill-feelings and unhappiness about her marriage and husband onto her children.

AFFIRMATION

In the midst of confusion I go within and seek my highest good.

---

* Catherine Ponder, *Open Your Mind to Receive* (Marina del Rey, CA: DeVorss, 1983).

DAY 317

A lot of people are trapped in convents [sic] just like a lot of women are trapped in marriages. They stay because they don't know what they'd do financially if they left. That's when the womb becomes a tomb, when you can't find the courage to leave what needs to be left.

SHERRY RUTH ANDERSON AND
PATRICIA HOPKINS*

Leaving home can be a metaphor for leaving a constricting place where we can no longer grow or live decently. Sherry Anderson and Patricia Hopkins remind us that men have always left home to find spiritual growth. However, they found that many spiritual women they interviewed did not have to leave home to find spirituality.

However, it is clearly not a good idea to stay home just because it's safe, or because we're scared to take financial responsibility.

AFFIRMATION

I find the courage to take care of myself financially.

---

* Sherry Ruth Anderson and Patricia Hopkins, *The Feminine Face of God: The Unfolding of the Sacred in Women* (New York: Bantam Books, 1991).

DAY 318

Money and power can liberate only if they're used to do so. They can imprison and inhibit more finally than barred windows and iron chains.

MAYA ANGELOU*

AFFIRMATION

I know why I want money and what I will do with it.

---

* Maya Angelou, *Wouldn't Take Nothing for My Journey Now* (New York: Random House, 1993).

DAY 319

All change is a miracle to contemplate; but it is a miracle which is taking place every instant

ATTRIBUTED TO HENRY DAVID THOREAU

AFFIRMATION

I willingly surrender to the changes in my life.

Sheelah Ryan knew exactly what she wanted to do with the $55.2 million jackpot she had just won. "I want to set up a foundation to help the elderly and the abused women with children."

TAIT TRUSSELL*

Three months after she won the jackpot, the Sheelah Ryan Foundation was in operation and Sheelah was overseeing it. When the act of doling out money to abused women kept those women coming back for more, the foundation started buying houses (nine so far) "where abused women can live temporarily while they are encouraged to get further education and training that can make them self-reliant."

When Sheelah Ryan won her millions, she lived alone in a double-wide mobile home, sold real estate, and was saving to replace an aging Mercury. When asked about her personal philosophy she says, "I have always given something back to society. Now I happen to have more money."

AFFIRMATIONS

- *I help myself by helping others.*
- *As I receive so I give back.*

---

* Tait Trussell, "Leaving It All to Chance," *AARP Bulletin,* December 1990.

The possibility is that people are where they are because there is simply no way out for them. We begin to see that personal power breeds personal success and that success breeds personal power.

JOAN CHITTISTER*

AFFIRMATION

I maximize my personal power for my own success and to help others.

* Joan Chittister, *Job's Daughters: Women and Power* (Mahwah, NJ: Paulist Press, 1990).

DAY 322

Let's be clear on the fact that tobacco and alcohol are killing more people than cocaine. It's time for consumers to speak out and put a stop to the marketing of sickness and death to our children.

MARIAN WRIGHT EDELMAN*

The bad habits of our living can cost us and our loved ones enormous sums of money, not to mention our lives.

Exercise: Look at your overall life pattern and start to change negatives to positives.

AFFIRMATION
I lovingly root out the addictions and bad habits that harm me and others.

---

* Marian Wright Edelman, *The Measure of Our Success—A Letter to My Children and Yours* (Boston: Beacon Press, 1992).

DAY 323

Whatever the things are that would make your life more personally meaningful before you die—do them now, because you are going to die, and you may not have the time or energy when you get your final notice.

ELISABETH KUBLER-ROSS*

Exercise: Consider what would make your life more personally meaningful, and do it now.

AFFIRMATION
Today offers opportunities to make my life more personally meaningful.

---

* Elisabeth Kubler-Ross, *Death: The Final Stage of Growth* (Englewood Cliffs, NJ: Prentice-Hall, 1975)

Am I willing to make a living without having a job: Am I willing to go against Conventional Wisdom? To make lifestyle changes? To make personal sacrifices? To do my homework and to learn from other self-bossers? To commit to a path that offers no guarantees of success? To fail in order ultimately to succeed? To trust myself more? To keep going until I accomplish my goals? To accept money for having fun?

BARBARA J. WINTER*

Exercise: If self-employment is your goal, explore possibilities and go for it.

AFFIRMATION

I am willing to make lifestyle changes in order to achieve my financial and personal goals.

---

* Barbara J. Winter, *Making a Living Without a Job: Winning Ways for Creating Work That You Love* (New York: Bantam, 1993).

DAY 325

The only other rule worth knowing about money is: take it any time anyone wants to put it into your hands.

ALICE KOLLER*

AFFIRMATION

I am able to receive financial gifts without duty or obligation.

---

* Alice Koller, *The Stations of Solitude* (New York: Bantam, 1990).

DAY 326

Suddenly I decided not to run away from it any longer, but to meet it head on.

JAN DE HARTOG*

Sooner or later we all face what we want to run from. You can turn around now and face it flamboyantly; you can do it slowly and by degrees; or you can wait for change to catch you unprepared.

AFFIRMATION

I am strong enough now to face what I have run from.

---

* Jan de Hartog, *The Hospital* (New York: Atheneum, 1964).

To discover what your real needs are in preparation for stepping off the fast track, begin by scrutinizing what you currently spend money on. Chart a few months worth of past bills and expenses to see clearly your pattern of spending habits. Be as thorough as you can—no item is too small to mention.

M. M. KIRSCH*

AFFIRMATION

I enjoy learning how I spend money and directing and controlling that spending.

---

*M. M. Kirsch, *How to Get Off the Fast Track and Live a Life Money Can't Buy* (New York: HarperPaperbacks, 1991).

DAY 328

Success can make you go one of two ways. It can make you a prima donna, or it can smooth the edges, take away the insecurities, let the nice things come out.

JEAN WARD-JONES[*]

AFFIRMATION

I am a successful woman and I feel good about myself!

---

[*] Jean Ward-Jones, *Woman to Woman* (Memphis, TN: Impressions Ink, 1993).

So long as we see ourselves as essentially separate, competitive, and ego-identified beings, it is difficult to respect the validity of our social despair, deriving as it does from interconnectedness. Both our capacity to grieve for others and our power to cope with this grief spring from the great matrix of relationships in which we take our being. We are, as open systems, sustained by flows of energy and information that extends beyond the reach of conscious ego.

JOANNA MACY*

AFFIRMATION

Because of the interconnectedness of all life I have impact and must take responsibility for the way I generate financial winning.

---

*Joanna Macy, *World As Lover, World As Self* quoted in *Yoga Journal*, January/February 1992.

DAY 330

You have to believe in yourself and then you can be merciful with everybody. I think this is what Jesus said.

MARIA RIFO*

A surprising number of women have money and don't know what to do with it. They are imprisoned by their wealth. As Gloria Steinem says in *Moving Beyond Words:* "Most of the wealthy widows I'd heard so much about—the basis of the belief that 'women control the economy'—turned out to be conduits for passing power to children, especially to sons and sons-in-law.... The real money and decision making powers were consigned to unbreakable trusts and to family trustees who were generally paternalistic, often condescending, and occasionally corrupt. I met only one widow who was in control of her own financial life, and she had spent several hard years getting there."

AFFIRMATION

I believe in myself and my ability to change and grow.

---

* Quoted in Sherry Ruth Anderson and Patricia Hopkins, *The Feminine Face of God* (New York: Bantam Books, 1991).

DAY 331

Unilateral power, no matter how well-intentioned, breeds insensitivity to whatever it touches. As long as we know what is good for the other, there is no reason to really get to know the other, or to listen to the other, or to learn from the other....

Integrative power assumes that each of us has a power that is needed by the other and then sets [us] out to work together, as equals....

JOAN CHITTISTER[*]

Our goal of financial independence will probably lead us directly into contact with both unilateral and integrative power. We are wise to be prepared.

Exercise: Think hard about power in all your financial relationships. How are you using it? How are you being used?

AFFIRMATION
My financial relationships are built on integrative power.

---

[*] Joan Chittister, *Job's Daughters: Women and Power* (Mahwah, NJ: Paulist Press, 1990).

This woman discovered something we must all discover: In those quiet periods of growth, there first comes inner individual growth. Then comes outer growth and expansion in our affairs. How often we have tried to reverse the process!

CATHERINE PONDER*

AFFIRMATION

I learn to allow time to integrate my growth before I act upon it.

---

* Catherine Ponder, *Open Your Mind to Receive* (Marina del Rey, CA: DeVorss, 1983).

For the majority of women I spoke with, the issue that preoccupies them is not the lack of caring relationships but the shortcomings of those they are in. Most have a mate and children, but they find that something is missing at the heart of their relationships. Today their liberation has allowed them to ask for it. The problem is that men seem unable to supply them with the kind of emotional support they crave.

SUZANNE GORDON[*]

AFFIRMATION

I create many relationships of emotional support, above and beyond my primary relationship.

---

[*] Suzanne Gordon, *Prisoners of Men's Dreams: Striking Out for a New Feminine Future* (Boston: Little, Brown, 1991).

DAY 334

My opinion is that we must lend ourselves to others and give ourselves only to ourselves. If my will happened to be prone to mortgage and apply itself, I wouldn't last: I am too tender, both by nature and by practice.

MONTAIGNE*

   Who do you lend yourself to, and who and what do you give yourself to?

AFFIRMATION

I belong to myself, emotionally and financially.

---

* *Selections from the Essays of Michel Eyquem de Montaigne,* trans. and ed. by Donald M. Frame (New York: Appleton-Century, 1948).

The voice of the deep feminine is beginning to speak clearly and firmly to many women. And it is by sharing our inner truths, our sacred truths, with each other that a "new way," an untraditional perspective about what it means to live an embodied spirituality in the world today, is beginning to take form.

SHERRY RUTH ANDERSON AND
PATRICIA HOPKINS*

How can we know how to deal with money and daily life without understanding our values and their spiritual underpinnings?

AFFIRMATION

I find a way to give expression to my spirituality. I search until I find a path that is right for me.

---

* Sherry Ruth Anderson and Patricia Hopkins, *The Feminine Face of God: The Unfolding of the Sacred in Women* (New York: Bantam Books, 1991).

DAY 336

He told me once that sometimes we must look away from hard things and pray, before we turn back and do them.

NATALIE KUSZ[*]

AFFIRMATION

I am willing to "ask for help" and to work hard toward creating my financial future.

---

[*] Natalie Kusz, *Road Song* (New York: Farrar, Straus & Giroux, 1990).

Have you been able to think out and manage your own life? You have done the greatest task of all.

MONTAIGNE*

Why do we want to manage money? So we can better manage our lives. What keeps us from managing money and our lives? Often, we are resistant to change. It is a great day when we are finally free to look at the way we live unblinkingly and say: "I created this. If I don't like it, I can change it. I can look at every problem and ask, 'What must I learn and do to be free from this?'"

AFFIRMATIONS

- *True financial progress can begin with learning to manage my life— including my resistance to change.*
- *I love myself enough to tell myself the truth and face my resistance to change.*

---

* *Selections from the Essays of Michel Eyquem de Montaigne*, ed. and trans. by Donald M. Frame (New York: Appleton-Century, 1948).

DAY 338

Prosperity should no longer be regarded so much as a matter of politics and economics, but more as a matter of increased understanding and growth. True abundance on all levels of life comes as a result of developing a prosperous consciousness.

CATHERINE PONDER*

Catherine Ponder believes we must deliberately open our minds to receive because "most of us have endured a pinched, narrow existence for no good reason."

Think of the last time you denied yourself something when you didn't need to. Remember, many women are more accustomed to giving out than they are to taking in. Where do you stand on the continuum of giving and receiving? Keep track of your giving and receiving for a few days. Does your money and energy support people who don't support you? Do you give away support and attention you should be spending on yourself? You can give yourself permission to change these patterns if you want to.

Exercise: Review how comfortable you are with receiving. Do you think it is always better to give than to receive?

AFFIRMATION

I learn from my past, staying focused in the present, while I continue moving toward a solid financial future.

---

*Catherine Ponder, *Open Your Mind to Receive* (Marina del Rey, CA: DeVorss, 1983).

"I tried all kinds of tricks," another woman will say, "smoking substitutes, pills, poisoned cigarettes, not going to cocktail parties...all delaying tactics. Finally I got sick of it and asked myself straight out, 'Listen, you jerk! Do you mean it or not?' Then I meant it, and then I stopped."

ALLEN WHEELIS*

There is a story that goes like this: A woman is on the roof of her house in a flood. A canoe goes by; the people ask if they can help. "No," comes the reply, "The Lord will save me." A motorboat arrives to help her, and she says, "The Lord will save me." Finally a helicopter flies by only to receive the same refusal. "No, the Lord will save me."

The woman dies and goes to heaven's gates, where she screams at the Lord, "Why didn't you save me?"

The Lord says, "What do you want? First I sent a canoe, then a motorboat...."

We all have canoes, motorboats, and helicopters going by, carrying our financial possibilities. We use all sorts of delaying tactics to keep ourselves from getting the financial independence we want. We can stop using the delaying tactics and take those boats and helicopters!

AFFIRMATION

I decide what to do next and I do it.

---

* Allen Wheelis, *How People Change* (New York: Harper & Row, 1970).

Other people call it an unconscious or "direct knowing" ability, and it is usually accomplished in the most efficient and economical way possible. It gets you to the right place at the right time to be with the right people to do the right thing....I had to be willing to make a mistake, take a wrong turn, become anxious that I was lost or wasting time. I had to be willing to know that I don't know everything consciously.

JANET LEE MITCHELL*

AFFIRMATION

I open myself to unexpected ways of making money.

---

*Janet Lee Mitchell, *Conscious Evolution* (New York: Ballantine Books, 1989).

DAY 341

When the desire for "financial independence" grows excessive, it may breed illusions of self-sufficiency and thereby fuel the error of egoistic pride.

JACOB NEEDLEMAN*

Why do we want money? Are we like children playing in a gigantic sandbox, attempting to pile up more than anyone else? And what will we have proven when we do?

One day as I played in my money sandbox I realized that money for money's sake was ultimately as boring and as pointless as the childhood card game of war where the highest card always wins. My job then was to make money for my company by paying my part-time workers frugally while billing our clients steeply. If I did my job as well as I could (which, in my limited thinking of that time, I was duty bound to do), then I would ruthlessly play upon my employees' needs for work, money, and appreciation.

I could not stay in this terrifying space. Shortly thereafter, I went back to school.

AFFIRMATION

I know why I want financial independence, and what I will do with it.

---

*Jacob Needleman, *Money and the Meaning of Life* (New York: Doubleday, 1991).

If only someone had told me to stop—to wait—to let myself grieve. That's the best advice. I've only now, much belatedly, realized how much damage I've done.

LYNN CAINE*

The damage Lynn Caine talks about in *Being a Widow* is that of making major decisions too soon after the death of her husband. From a position of disorientation, Lynn further uprooted her life, taking action when she should have waited and healed. Elisabeth Kubler-Ross tells us there are stages of grief—getting over denial and accepting a new reality are major hurdles. We need time to take them.

AFFIRMATION

I plan now for the emotional support I will need during times of transition.

---

* Lynn Caine, *Being a Widow* (New York: William Morrow, 1988).

DAY 343

"You never know," Lettice said. "You never know in life, which is good experience and which is damage. Do you?"

JOANNA TROLLOPE[*]

You may never know your constructive experiences from the damaging ones until later—sometimes a long time later. When I consider the five years I wasted in a miserable marriage, I feel regret. Yet, so often, the thought of those wasted five years has been enough to tip me into needed action. And my long years of financial ignorance only make me more determined to better understand and manage my present financial life.

AFFIRMATION

I learn from my past, staying focused in the present, while I continue moving toward a solid financial future.

---

[*] Joanna Trollope, *A Village Affair* (New York: Harper & Row, 1989).

DAY 344

In the first place if power can be defined as the ability to shape the world according to your personal point of view, then women do not have power at all. At best, they may have moral suasion over those willing to be persuaded by them. They can only hope and, of course, pray.

JOAN CHITTISTER*

Prayer can take a long time to take effect. Women are waking up to find that Goddess helps those who help themselves—and that includes financially. They're saying, "This is my world. I can make changes that count."

AFFIRMATION

I utilize my personal power to create positive outcomes for my world.

---

* Joan Chittister, *Job's Daughters: Women and Power* (Mahwah, NJ: Paulist Press, 1990).

DAY 345

As tobacco companies lose revenues because so many smokers are kicking the habit, they're increasingly targeting young women, who they see as the most promising new market to replace traditionally older, male smokers.

DONNA JACKSON*

In the past five years, lung cancer has surpassed breast cancer as the number-one cancer killer of women. Currently, says Donna Jackson, 20 percent of high school women are carrying the deadly time bomb of a personal cigarette habit. How much will their lifetime (now reduced) of smoking cost them? How much will it cost society?

This cynicism of putting money and profits before human lives and suffering makes us angry. What can we do? Target magazines by writing letters to the editors, thanking those who don't carry cigarette advertising and telling those who do exactly why you're canceling your subscription. Ask your friends to do the same thing. The cost of smoking is an ongoing personal debit that no wise woman will pay.

Exercise: Buy for a friend or donate to a high school library: *Women Smokers Can Quit: A Different Approach.* Order 1-800-543-3854.

AFFIRMATION

I am making the world a better place for women.

---

*Donna Jackson, *How to Make the World a Better Place for Women in Five Minutes a Day* (New York: Hyperion, 1992).

Tithing is a way of showing gratitude for whoever or whatever you feel is responsible for the gift of life. It's paying your rent to live in this world. It's your share of the air you breathe, the color of the trees, the sun in the morning and the moon at night. It's also a most tangible way of saying, "Thank you. I have more than I need."

JOHN-ROGER AND PETER McWILLIAMS*

I'm learning to pay for the gift of life and it gives a joyous boost to my heart—I believe I actually feel it grow warmer. In contrast to my usual bargain-down tactics, sometimes I pay up. In contrast to looking out for myself, sometimes I put myself in another's shoes. The other night in a favorite bistro, I left double the price of my bill for a tip. The young waitress is working her way through nursing school. My generous tip was meant to encourage someone who works to help herself.

AFFIRMATION
As prosperity enters my life, I pass it on and empower others.

---

* John-Roger and Peter McWilliams, *Wealth 101: Getting What You Want— Enjoying What You've Got* (Los Angeles: Prelude Press, 1992).

DAY 347

"Why do you want to dance?" Without missing a beat, she gives him the answer, the only answer, "Why do you want to live?"

FROM THE MOVIE THE RED SHOES[*]

We cheat ourselves when we don't find our real work—not that it's always easy to do so. I had gone through two careers, earned a Ph.D. and passed forty when I found my real work of writing. I'm thankful now I kept pushing myself until I made this discovery. In *The Stations of Solitude*, Alice Koller makes an excellent distinction between *work* (we may or may not be paid for it) and a *job* (what we do to earn money to live). "With a job," she says, "you're letting someone else place a value on your time. With work, you set the value for your time.

AFFIRMATION

My greatest wealth comes from being true to myself.

---

[*] Quoted in Suzanne Farrell, *Holding on to the Air: An Autobiography* (New York: Summit Books, 1990).

Whatever we'd brought we used up completely, for it would have seemed unfaithful somehow to save anything, to arrive back home still holding a part of what we had promised ourselves we could squander.

NATALIE KUSZ[*]

AFFIRMATION

I always have something to squander.

---

[*] Natalie Kusz, *Road Song* (New York: Farrar, Straus & Giroux, 1990).

352

In the sixteenth century…St. Theresa said to her Novices, "Christ has no body on earth now except yours. No hands but yours, no feet but yours. Yours are the eyes through which His love has to look out upon the world. Yours are the feet on which He has to go about doing good. And yours are the hands with which He is to bless us now."

JAN DE HARTOG*

If you accept yourself as a handmaiden for spirituality, however you define it, then does it not necessarily follow that you must do the best you can with who and what you are? And is not your financial responsibility included among your stewardship and duties?

Exercise: Just for today stop trying so hard to manage your money and ponder the ways money brings joy to your life.

AFFIRMATIONS

- *I am a spiritual being who can enjoy being human.*
- *I allow my spirituality to be a life-affirming, earth-centered expression of joy.*

---

*Jan de Hartog, *The Lamb's War* (New York: Fawcett, 1980).

DAY 350

There are no mothers or fathers for grown-ups, only sisters and brothers.

SHELDON KOPP*

You may catch yourself making someone into an expert whose opinion is more valuable than yours. You may allow your financial advisor to make an investment that goes against your gut feeling or a physician to make an important decision about your body that you live to regret. We all have to learn to give greater value to our own informed opinions.

AFFIRMATION

There are no shortcuts to becoming my own best authority.

---

*Sheldon Kopp, *If You Meet the Buddha on the Road, Kill Him!* (New York: Bantam Books, 1972).

DAY 351

"Remember, Tochka," he tells me, "after all the long work, we have what we need. We never were called to build kingdoms." It's an old phrase of his, those words about kingdoms, and he has spoken it for years, since before our move north, before my accident, before the thousand substitutions of new plans for old. My father means, and the rest of us concur, that hopes are white stones shining up from the bottoms of pools, and every clear day we reach in up to the shoulder, selecting a few and rearranging the others...

NATALIE KUSZ[*]

I do what I can, I tell myself, meaning that when times are hard, materially or psychologically, I do little or nothing in the outside world. When times are good, I expand my perimeters by helping outhers.

AFFIRMATION

I practice ways of keeping hope and dreams alive through the dark days.

---

[*] Natalie Kusz, *Road Song* (New York: Farrar, Straus & Giroux, 1990).

DAY 352

...one can have certainties for years and then one day it dawns that one has been all wrong and just humbly [has] to start from zero and try to do better.

Nicolas Freeling*

When one path turns out to be wrong for me I am not afraid to try a different path.

Affirmation

I welcome the insights that change my financial path.

---

* Nicolas Freeling, *Not As Far As Velma* (New York: Warner Books, 1990).

DAY 353

To bring the quality of simplicity into our levels and patterns of consumption, we must learn to live between the extremes of poverty and excess. Simplicity is a double-edged sword in this regard...too much or too little diminish[es] our capacity to realize our human potentials.

DUANE ELGIN*

Voluntary simplicity is easy for me; to do my work all I really require is paper, pen, solitude, and a public library. My computer, which I adore for its efficiency, could be sacrificed or viewed as paying its way by enhanced production. Technology can trip us or it can help us. We must negotiate and renegotiate our middle path.

AFFIRMATION

I move toward the quality of simplicity as a means of realizing my financial potential.

---

* Duane Elgin, *Voluntary Simplicity: Toward a Way of Life That Is Outwardly Simple, Inwardly Rich* (New York: William Morrow, 1981).

DAY 354

An exceptional friend, a devout, twenty-year meditator, says she can no longer watch movies or TV shows when meanness, violence or pornography are dramatized.

MARSHA SINETAR[*]

More and more women now refuse to support violence. They will not spend their money on violent movies or books. For example, people in my town have banded together to boycott a movie theater where the manager raped a woman and did not receive adequate punishment. Even a year later women tell me, "I never go to that theater."

AFFIRMATION

I use the "power of the purse" to support women.

---

[*] Marsha Sinetar, *A Way Without Words: A Guide for Spiritually Emerging Adults* (Mahwah, NJ: Paulist Press, 1992).

Knowing how to feel satisfied with few possessions helps us avoid buying unnecessarily and becoming part of an economic system that exploits others, and it enables us to decrease our involvement in the pollution of our environment.

THICH NHAT HANH[*]

Our earth is a small and contained environment. Every individual's financial and economic decisions have impact on that person and other people and on the fragile environment we all share.

AFFIRMATION

I recognize the interconnectedness of our world and I manage my life accordingly.

---

[*] Thich Nhat Hanh, *The Sutra on the Eight Realizations of the Great Beings: A Buddhist Scripture on Simplicity, Generosity and Compassion* (Berkeley, CA: Parallax Press, 1987).

DAY 356

Expect the best:
   convert problems into opportunities:
Be dissatisfied with the status quo;
   Focus on where you want to go,
      instead of where you're coming from
and most importantly,
      Decide to be happy.
         Knowing it's an attitude,
            a habit gained from daily practice,
               and not a result or payoff.

DENIS WAITLEY*

AFFIRMATIONS

- *I have decided to be happy and put into practice what I already know.*
- *Each day I become happier and happier.*

---

* Quoted in Susan Hayward, *A Guide for the Advanced Soul* (Crows Nest, Australia: In-Tune Books, 1985).

DAY 357

The dictionary defines serendipity as "the faculty of making fortunate and unexpected discoveries by accident." This means that while you are in the process of trying to achieve something, you encounter an unexpected turn-of-events that causes you to achieve something better, greater, and more fortunate than you were looking for in the first place.

WILLIAM HEWITT*

AFFIRMATION

I open to serendipitous financial encounters.

* William Hewitt, *Bridges to Success and Fulfillment* (St. Paul, MN: Llewellyn, 1993).

DAY 358

Himsha closed her eyes and sat quite still. In that stillness, during which she seemed to be suspended in space, some small strength, some beginning of a new, serene power began to communicate itself to her. It grew within her, it seemed to fill her slowly with an unemotional tranquility, a stillness that was not silence but fullness of light, growing awareness of the reality of the infinite ocean of light and love that was God, which now communicated itself to her and needed her to communicate itself to those solid women in their bowler hats, squatting on the edge of infinity, their dying babies in their laps.

JAN DE HARTOG*

Himsha, a South American Indian, was saved as a baby by a woman who went on to become a physician serving children—raising money to feed them and move them to places of safety. In this passage, she has just been killed trying to lead a planeload of African children to safety. Himsha, although she has not yet heard of the death of her mentor, does know at a deeper level—and is taking up her mentor's task.

AFFIRMATION

I make spaces so I may hear the silence within, and how I am called to service.

---

*Jan de Hartog, *The Lamb's War* (New York: Fawcett, 1980).

362

DAY 359

In the long run we shape our lives and we shape ourselves. The process never ends until we die. And the choices we make are ultimately our own responsibility.

ELEANOR ROOSEVELT[*]

AFFIRMATION

I love taking responsibility for myself.

[*] Quoted in A. Cusick, *Choices: What Am I Doing With My Life?* (Sydney, Australia: Simon & Schuster Australia, 1990).

DAY 360

I am entitled to miracles.

A Course in Miracles*

Affirmation

I feel good about myself and that includes my financial life.

* *A Course in Miracles,* (Glen Ellen, CA: Foundation for Inner Peace, 1975).

DAY 361

If we give from the joy of thanksgiving, with a heart full of gratitude, then we will receive back in joy, thanksgiving and gratitude. People will not just give you what is yours; they will thank you for being in their lives. Tithing is a physical affirmation of both abundance and gratitude. The more abundant and grateful you feel as you give your tithe, the wealthier you will be.

JOHN-ROGER AND PETER MCWILLIAMS[*]

One step of any twelve-step program asks you to make a list of all the people you owe because you've hurt them with your behavior. Then you must contact each person you hurt and sincerely apologize for the harm you did.

When our finances take an upward turn perhaps that's a time to examine our pasts for unresolved debts and to give appropriate gifts to those who have helped us.

AFFIRMATION

Each day I give thanks for all that I have been given and I gratefully give of myself to my friends.

---

[*] John-Roger and Peter McWilliams, *Wealth 101: Getting What You Want— Enjoying What You've Got* (Los Angeles, CA: Prelude Press, 1992).

DAY 362

The non-Moneyphobic women in our study enjoyed making, spending, and investing, and took pleasure in their financial independence.
The few non-Moneyphobic women we found were happy women.

ANNETTE LIEBERMAN AND VICKI LINDNER*

Happiness can be the reward for getting your financial life in order and for learning what money means to you. You enjoy money. You have enough for yourself. You own money instead of letting money own you. You've also learned how to integrate money and relationships in healthy ways. You have taken responsibility for taking care of yourself. You are a financially independent woman, or happily on your way to becoming one.

AFFIRMATION

I am living the financial life I want, and I love it!

---

* Annette Lieberman and Vicki Lindner, *Unbalanced Accounts: How Women Can Overcome Their Fear of Money* (New York: Penguin Books, 1987).

DAY 363

You have to make room for your prosperity to come to you...if you make a place for prosperity in your life, it will appear in increasing amounts. ...It is not until we recognize our union with all aspects of the universal source that we begin to grasp the meaning of prosperity—unlimited substance....

Money is a good place to practice the shift from ideas of lack and limitation to those of connectedness with infinite source. Universal substance is always available in invisible form and able to provide us with everything we need in any form we choose.

JANET LEE MITCHELL[*]

AFFIRMATION

I release all thoughts of lack and limitation and create space for prosperity in my life.

---

[*] Janet Lee Mitchell, *Conscious Evolution* (New York: Ballantine Books, 1989).

DAY 364

Principle 5: Do Not Be Afraid of Monetary Self-Interest. The overriding principle in Taoism is that we must learn to use the natural forces of the universe to achieve our goals. Learning to find the way of least resistance is the key.

IVAN HOFFMAN*

AFFIRMATION

The universe supports me in achieving my financial goals.

---

* Ivan Hoffman, *The Tao of Money: Six Simple Principles for Achieving Financial Harmony* (Rocklin, CA: Prima Publishing, 1994).

DAY 365

You are one of the most fortunate women ever. As an American woman today, you can expect to enjoy an abundance of years all but unprecedented in the history of the world. You can plan on nearly one-third more retirement years than men of your age. Compared to your great-grandmother, you have a full second lifetime to enjoy—a kind of rebirth. What the caesars and queens of history couldn't buy with all their power you've got a shot at—one more chance. And with the proper planning, you can make your second life even better than the first. You have a giant head start.

FRANCES LEONARD*

AFFIRMATION

Now is the time for me to begin my new, full lifetime.

---

* Frances Leonard, *Women and Money: The Independent Woman's Guide to Financial Security for Life* (New York: Addison-Wesley, 1991).

RESOURCES

Here is a short list of highly readable and helpful books for your further exploration. Although they are placed in broad categories here, many of these books transcend category and address more than one of the most vital issues surrounding women and their money.

AFFIRMATIONS / EMPOWERMENT

James Fadiman, *Unlimit Your Life: Setting and Getting Goals* (Berkeley, CA: Celestial Arts, 1989).

Max Gunther, *How to Get Lucky* (New York: Stein & Day, 1986).

Louise L. Hay, *You Can Heal Your Life* (Santa Monica, CA: Hay House, 1984).

Alan Lakein, *How to Get Control of Your Time and Your Life* (New York: NAL-Dutton, 1989).

Phil Laut, *Money Is My Friend* (New York: Ivy Books, 1990).

Marilyn Mason, *Making Our Lives Our Own: A Woman's Guide to the Six Challenges of Personal Change* (New York: Harper Collins, 1991).

Lee Morical, *Where's My Happy Ending? Women and the Myth of Having It All* (Reading, MA: Addison-Wesley, 1984).

Maya Pilkington, *The Real-Life Aptitude Test: How to Find Out What You Want—and Get It!* (New York: Pharos Books, 1987).

Attitudes Toward Money

Alexandra Armstrong and Mary R. Donahue, *On Your Own: A Widow's Passage to Emotional and Financial Well-Being* (Dearborn, MI: Financial Publishing, 1993).

Anne DeSola Cardoza and Mavis B. Sutton, *Winning Tactics for Women Over Forty* (Bedford, MA: Mills and Sanderson, 1988).

Victoria Felton-Collins, *Couples and Money: Why Money Interferes with Love and What to Do About It* (New York: Bantam Books, 1990).

Lois G. Forer, *What Every Woman Needs to Know Before (and After) She Gets Involved with Men and Money* (New York: Rawson Associates, 1993).

Donna Jackson, *How to Make the World a Better Place for Women in Five Minutes a Day* (New York: Hyperion, 1992).

Annette Lieberman and Vicki Linder, *Unbalanced Accounts: Why Women Are Still Afraid of Money* (New York: Penguin Books, 1988).

Frances Cerra Whittlesey, *Why Women Pay More: How to Avoid Marketplace Perils* (Washington, D.C.: Center for Study of Responsive Law, 1993).

FINANCIAL PLANNING AND BUSINESS

Adriane G. Berg, *Your Wealth Building Years: Financial Planning for 18 to 38 Year Olds* (New York: Newmarket Press, 1991).

Joan German-Grapes, *Ninety Days to Financial Fitness* (New York: Collier Books, 1993).

Joline Godfrey, *Our Wildest Dreams: Women Entrepreneurs Making Money, Having Fun, Doing Good* (New York: Harper Business, 1992).

Frances Leonard, *Women and Money at 40: The Independent Woman's Guide to Financial Security for Life* (New York: Addison-Wesley, 1991).

Judith A. Martindale and Mary J. Moses, *Creating Your Own Future: A Woman's Guide to Retirement Planning* (Naperville, IL: Source-books Trade, 1991).

Elisabeth Ruedy and Sue Nirenberg, *Where Do I Put the Decimal Point? How to Conquer Math Anxiety and Increase Your Facility with Numbers* (New York: Henry Holt, 1990).

Mary Elizabeth Schlayer, *How to Be Financially Secure* (New York: Ballantine, 1987).

ABUNDANCE

David Chilton, *The Wealthy Barber: The Common-Sense Guide to Becoming Financially Independent* (Rocklin, CA: Prima Publishing, 1991).

Joe Dominguez and Vicki Robin, *Your Money or Your Life: Transforming Your Relationship With Money and Achieving Financial Independence* (New York: Viking/Penguin, 1992).

Jerrold Mundis, *How to Get Out of Debt, Stay Out of Debt, and Live Prosperously* (New York: Bantam Books, 1988).

Jacob Needleman, *Money and the Meaning of Life: Transforming Your Relationship with Money and Achieving Financial Independence* (New York: Doubleday, 1991).

Stephen M. Pollan and Mark Levine, *The Business of Living* (New York: Simon & Schuster, 1991).

Catherine Ponder, *Open Your Mind to Receive* (Marina del Rey, CA: DeVorss, 1983).

Spirituality, Inspiration, and Psychology

Sherry Anderson and Patricia Hopkins, *The Feminine Face of God: The Unfolding of the Sacred in Women* (New York: Bantam Books, 1992).

Clarissa Pinkola Estés, *Women Who Run with the Wolves* (New York: Ballantine Books, 1992).

Susan Hayward, *A Guide for the Advanced Soul* (Crows Nest, Australia: In-Tune Books, 1985).

Barbara Sher and Annie Gottlieb, *Wishcraft: How to Get What You Really Want* (New York: Ballantine Books, 1986).

Florence Scovel Shinn, *The Game of Life and How to Play It* (Marina del Rey, CA: DeVorss, 1978).

Samuel J. Warner, *Self-Realization and Self-Defeat* (New York: Grove Press, 1966).

Allen Wheelis, *How People Change* (New York: Harper Collins, 1975).

Elizabeth Friar Williams, *Notes of a Feminist Therapist* (New York: Dell, 1976).